San Ramon CHRONICLES

By Beverly Lane
for the Museum of the San Ramon Valley

San Ramon Chronicles

Stories of Bygone Days

The History Press

Published by The History Press
Charleston, SC 29403
www.historypress.net

Front cover: This gasoline-powered, horse-pulled combined harvester belonged to Fred Wiedemann and was used in fields all over the San Ramon Valley to reap grain in the '20s and '30s. *Wiedemann collection*; A contemporary view looking northeast from the Wiedemann hills across San Ramon to Mount Diablo. *Wiedemann collection.*
Back cover: Pioneers pause for a photograph at a picnic about 1890. *Museum of the San Ramon Valley*; Owner Henry Hurst stands in front of his San Ramon General Store and post office in 1911. *Museum of the San Ramon Valley.*

First published 2015

Manufactured in the United States

ISBN 978.1.46711.843.9

Library of Congress Control Number: 2015943865

Contents

Acknowledgements

It has taken a village to produce this book about the historic San Ramon community and its late twentieth-century transformations. People have been unfailingly willing to help.

Many authors have written about San Ramon's history, in particular Irma M. Dotson, Virgie V. Jones, Roxanne Wiedemann Lindsay, Sandee Wiedemann, James D. Smith, Henry Wiedemann, Carmen Geldermann, Viola Lynch Jones and Rose Peters Emery. I am indebted to each of them. What they have written has enriched these chronicles and made them possible. The several comprehensive Contra Costa County histories published in 1879, 1882, 1917, 1926 and 1942 all provided excellent background as well.

Interviews enhanced all the essays, some done many years ago and some done recently. These include newspaper articles that provided some direct quotations as well as my own interviews reaching back to the 1990s. All are now in the archives of the Museum of the San Ramon Valley, readily available for future researchers.

Help from the City of San Ramon was much appreciated. Mayor Bill Clarkson was an enthusiastic supporter, and Phil Wong, Karen McNamara, Nicole Blazin and Renee Beck assisted in many ways. Mary Ann Wilkman and Jan Smith at Forest Home Farms Historic Park helped as well.

Most of the photographs came from the Museum of the San Ramon Valley. Ralph Cozine's assistance with these photographs and his writings on agriculture are very much appreciated. A word about the caricatures on playing cards: as part of the city's fifth anniversary in 1988, Diane

Schinnerer gathered pictures for the artist and produced a deck of cards with drawings of San Ramon leaders. A few of these appear in the modern essays to lighten the text.

Many thanks to people who read and edited these essays, in particular Joyce Gunn and Marillyn Cozine, who read them all. Others also read individual essays and assisted with fact-checking: Joe Covello, Mary Lou Oliver, Mike and Joyce Wahlig, Jeff Wiedemann, Sandee Wiedemann, Roxanne Lindsay, Don Wood, Nancy Kreiser, Diane and Don Schinnerer and Phil Wong. A very special thank-you to Vivienne Wong, whose sharp eye, editing pen and many substantive suggestions improved every part of the book.

And thank you again to my husband, Jim, for his unswerving support and understanding.

I hope you enjoy this glimpse into San Ramon's past.

Introduction

This book brings together San Ramon stories the author has researched and written about over the past twenty-five years, plus a few special newspaper articles and memoirs of early residents. It just scratches the surface of San Ramon's history. There is much more that could be written about this vibrant area and much more to be learned about its past.

That said, *San Ramon Chronicles* shares some core narratives all in one place. San Ramon's past reflects that of California, from its long Indian settlement to brief Spanish years and the Gold Rush from which most people recount the state's beginnings. In the nineteenth century, the area had an identity crisis with several names attached to it. But when the Southern Pacific's San Ramon Branch Line ended in San Ramon in 1891, the name San Ramon was firmly established.

Agriculture dominated the region until suburban development and a signature business park transformed San Ramon in the late twentieth century. After thirty years as an incorporated city, a new city center is expected to become the focus of a modern-day San Ramon with the new city hall not far away.

Touted as energetic and progressive, San Ramon has grown to nearly eighty thousand people from a tiny village just a century ago.

A Look at San Ramon

Beginnings

Today San Ramon is a dynamic community, the fourth-largest city in Contra Costa County. It has a variety of parks, homes, stores and a major employment center all in a setting of remarkable beauty.

Mount Diablo can be seen from nearly every point in San Ramon. A geologist's delight, it is a young mountain composed of very old rocks. The 3,489-foot mountain is composed of a jumble of rocks from the Franciscan formation that punched through the once-overlying Cretaceous and Miocene formations. In 1851, its summit became the reference point for U.S. land surveys in most of California and all of Nevada.

Ancient fossils are found at all elevations of the valley. The Blackhawk Ranch Fossil Quarry just northeast of San Ramon has biota that represents large animal and plant life from nine to ten million years ago, when the area was a savanna. Currently owned by the University of California's Museum of Paleontology in Berkeley, the quarry has yielded more than 3,400 specimens, including remnants of mastodons, saber-toothed cats, camels and sumac and mahogany trees.

Geologist Ron Crane has pointed out that the region is still active tectonically with future earthquakes on the Calaveras fault to be expected. Other faults listed in San Ramon General Plans are the Bollinger, Dublin and Pleasanton faults.

San Ramon was once home to Ohlone Indians who lived adjacent to the area's many creeks. After 1797, the region became Mission San Jose grazing

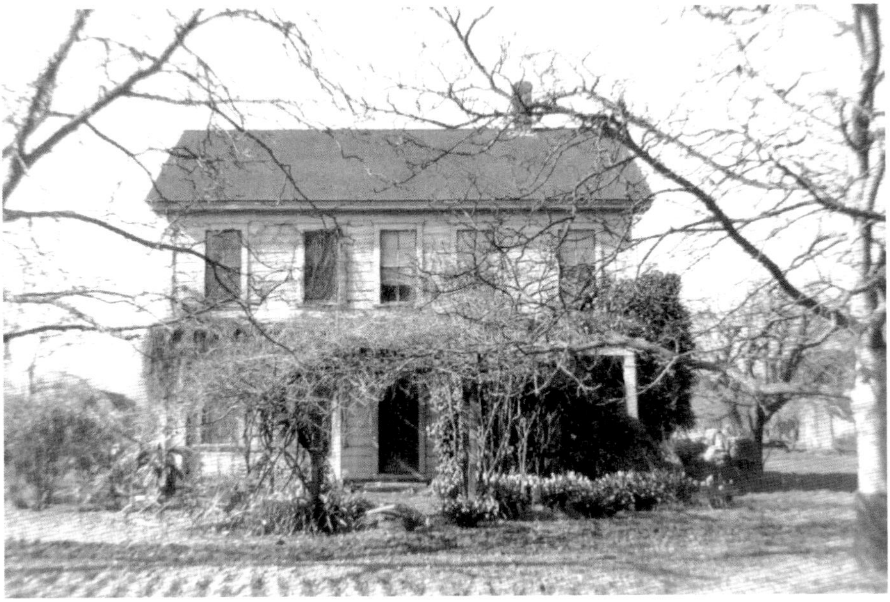

Original Norris home built by Leo Norris and carpenter William Lynch. It was the first wood-frame house in the San Ramon Valley and lasted a century, from 1850 to 1950. *Museum of the San Ramon Valley.*

land. Beginning in 1834, nearly all of San Ramon was part of Jose Maria Amador's twenty-thousand-plus-acre Rancho San Ramon. San Ramon Creek and Valley were named for a mission Indian, Ramon, who tended sheep here.

American settlers first arrived in late 1850 when Leo and Mary Jane Norris purchased 4,550 acres of land from Amador and built the first wood frame house in San Ramon. Other early pioneers were named Lynch, Dougherty, Harlan, Glass, Horan, Barrett, Brewen, Wiedemann and Fereira. Samuel Russell was the initial postmaster from 1852 to 1859.

Many of San Ramon's founding families are remembered because their names grace various landmarks. For instance, there are Bollinger, Crow and Norris Canyons, Thorup Lane, Dougherty Road, Brewin Lane and Wiedemann Hill.

A VILLAGE DEVELOPS

San Ramon Village began at a 490-foot elevation on the valley floor at the intersection of Deerwood Road, San Ramon Valley Boulevard and San Ramon Creek, marked today by a row of mature eucalyptus trees. The north–south road was first called the San Jose to Martinez road, then the county road or old highway, then State Highway 21 and finally San Ramon Valley Boulevard.

The village gradually became a hub of community activity with general stores, a school, saloons, hotels, a boot shop, blacksmith shops, laundries and a jail. In 1864, a stage line established by Brown and Co. ran from San Ramon through the valley to Oakland. San Ramon's permanent post office opened in 1873.

Nineteenth-century travel in and out of San Ramon took a long time and always involved horses. Henry Wiedemann wrote, "Taking San Francisco as a starting point, to go to San Ramon before the railroad, a fair average I would judge would be about 5 hours."

As its population grew, the village had a variety of names that reflected early settlers (Eli Brewen and William Lynch) and a large Irish population (Limerick). When the Southern Pacific's San Ramon Branch Line opened in 1891, the name "San Ramon" permanently replaced "Limerick" for the village.

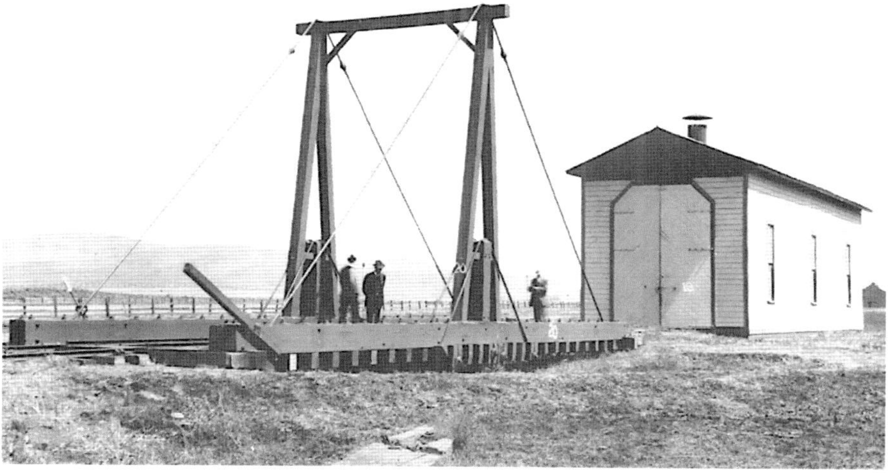

The San Ramon station included an engine house and a "gallows" turnaround. The San Ramon Branch Line ended in San Ramon until 1909, when it continued to Radum in Pleasanton. *Museum of the San Ramon Valley.*

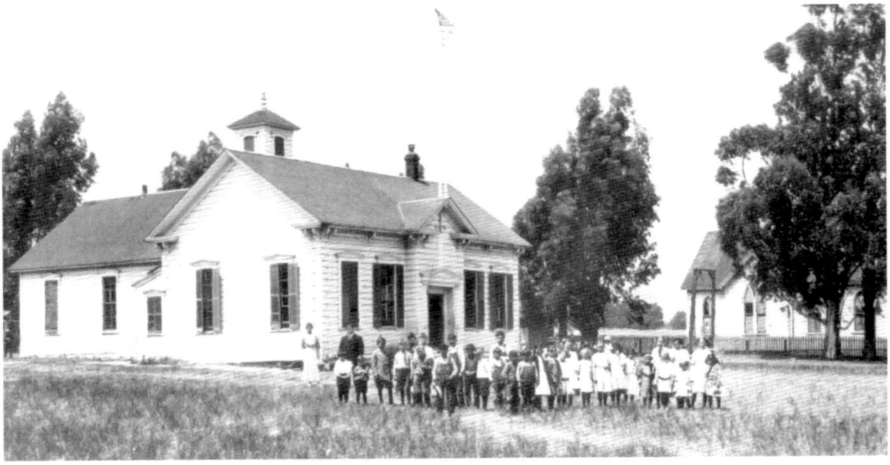

San Ramon Grammar School showing the Methodist church to the north. The entire student body is getting its picture taken here in the early 1900s. Blanch Wilson (the primary-grade teacher) and John McIver (the upper-grade teacher) stand near the school. *Museum of the San Ramon Valley.*

With the new train, crops and passengers could travel in and out of the area no matter what the weather. Until 1909 when the line extended south to Pleasanton, San Ramon was the branch line terminus and boasted a two-story depot, engine house and "gallows" turnaround. Visitors took a dirt road and a wooden bridge over San Ramon Creek to reach village establishments.

In 1895, attorney Thomas Bishop acquired one and a half square miles of Norris land and began a ranch on the valley floor. After he died in 1906, the Bishop Brothers Ranch grew to two thousand acres. The ranchers grazed cattle and planted hay, grain, diversified fruit crops and walnuts. The ranch's Shropshire purebred sheep earned numerous awards. Partially irrigated from an underground aquifer, at one point, the ranch included the world's largest single Bartlett pear orchard.

The San Ramon Hall was built in 1911 and became the community's social center, drawing ranch families to dances, school programs and plays for over fifty years. Residents belonged to several community groups over the years, including the Danville Grange No. 85, Odd Fellows, Farm Bureau, Ramona Club, Woodmen of the World, Temperance Cavaliers, San Ramon Public Hall Association, San Ramon Ladies Association, Ladies' Aide, Cattlemen's Association, San Ramon Women's Club and Mothers' Club.

San Ramon's general store was a fixture along the old highway in the twentieth century. As Carmen Geldermann recalled in 1939, "Much of the life of the community still breathed through the old store and post office—and what a store it was! At that time [early 1900s] Mr. Hurst ran it and one could [with patience] buy anything from a buggy whip to the horehound drops on the top shelf and meet half the countryside in the bargain."

MODERN SAN RAMON

As with the entire Tri-Valley, agriculture was the basis for San Ramon's economy. For years, a sign reading "San Ramon Pop. 100" reflected the number of people in the area. The entire San Ramon Valley had around two thousand people for the first half of the twentieth century.

Suburban development was spurred by the I-680 freeway, which went through San Ramon to Dublin in late 1966. In 1960, San Ramon did not appear separately in the census. The designation "San Ramon Village" appeared in the 1970 census with a count of over four thousand people, which reflected new homes built by developers Kenneth Volk and Robert McLain in South San Ramon and Dublin.

Western Electric purchased 1,733 acres of the Bishop Ranch in 1969 and proposed a "new town" that would include housing, parks, stores and controlled manufacturing facilities. This plan sparked development in north San Ramon as hundreds of homes were built. In 1978, Sunset Development Company purchased 585 acres, which became today's premier Bishop Ranch Business Park.

During this transition from rural to suburban communities, the San Ramon Homeowners Association, Homeowners Association of Twin Creeks,

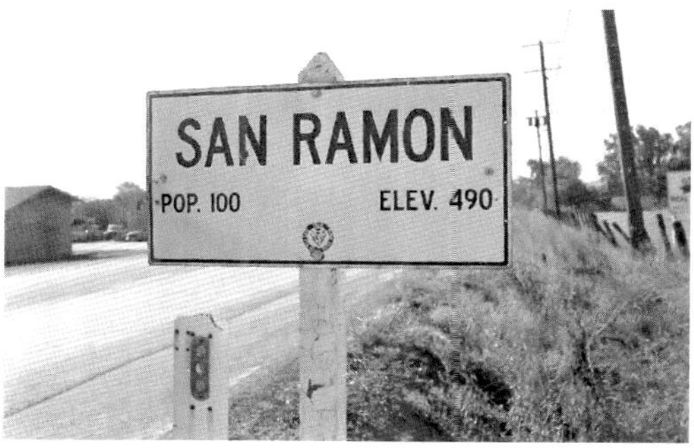

This San Ramon sign on State Highway 21 across from the Brass Door stood there for years even when the population had grown well beyond one hundred. *Museum of the San Ramon Valley.*

Greater San Ramon Improvement Association and San Ramon Valley Chamber of Commerce represented San Ramon's interests at the county.

On March 8, 1983, San Ramon voted to incorporate as a new city, taking control of development, police, parks and municipal services for the area. New community centers, theaters, Olympic-size pools, a museum, numerous parks, a community college and a hospital testify to the accomplishments of the modern city. Its pastoral period is featured at Forest Home Farms Historic Park. In 2016, a distinctive new city hall will open.

San Ramon grew dramatically after 1970 into the community it is today. In 1960, it had an estimated 300 people; in 1970, 4,084 people; in 1980, 22,356; in 2000, 44,722; in 2010, 72,148; and in 2014, 78,820. No longer a quiet rustic edge of the East Bay, San Ramon looks to the future and values its past.

First People: The Ohlone Indians

For untold centuries, people have lived in San Ramon. They built their homes by the creeks, hunted in the valley and worshipped on the mountain. The Ohlone tribes of Souyen and Seunen inhabited this area when the Spanish first arrived in 1772.

The First People

They called themselves "The People." Today, we call them Indians or Native Americans. While little information remains about the local Indians' specific culture, they would have had an intimate relationship with the land, a cycle of life that changed very gradually from generation to generation and a tribal organization that owned the rights to hunt, fish, gather and pray within clearly designated territories.

Living in village communities of fifty to two hundred people, the rhythm of their lives was determined by one harvest or another. The Bay Area and the San Ramon Valley provided an infinite variety of foods. The Indians collected acorns, nuts and seeds; hunted birds, deer and elk; and caught fish.

They expanded their food resources by trading with other groups. For instance, they traded with coastal groups such as the Carquin or Jalquin, exchanging acorns and local seeds for seafood like abalone, oysters, salmon

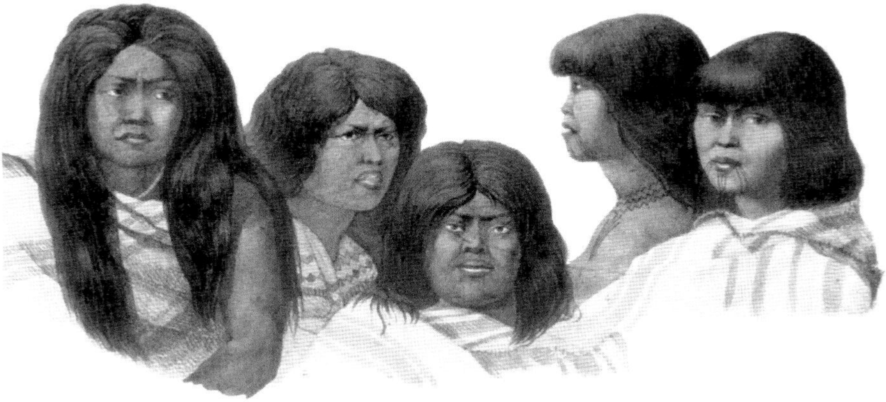

A drawing of Bay Area Indians in 1806 by artist Louis Choris. *The Bancroft Library.*

and sturgeon. At other times, larger groups met for feasts and dances, probably at places near today's Danville Oak or at autumn festivals on Mount Diablo.

Living in the Watersheds

The watersheds in which Indians lived provided a cornucopia of rich food resources. Stephen Powers in the 1870s wrote about tribal knowledge of its territories:

> *The boundaries of all tribes are marked out with the greatest precision, being defined by certain creeks, canyons, boulders, conspicuous trees, springs, etc., each of which has its individual name...* [The mothers] *teach these things to their children...Over and over, time and again they rehearse all these boundaries, describing each minutely and by name, with its surroundings...If any Indian knows but little of this great world more than pertains to boundary bush and boulder, he knows his own small fighting ground intimately better than any topographical engineer can learn it.*

California tribal boundaries generally followed watersheds, which extended from hill and mountain ridges and led to creeks. When travelers wanted to cross tribal lands, they were expected to recognize these boundaries and request permission to enter.

San Ramon Indians lived in the headwaters of the Alhambra Creek Watershed, which drains from Mount Diablo. Today's names for the creeks are South San Ramon, Coyote, East and West Alamo and Tassajara. People lived along the small streams and springs either permanently or seasonally.

SACRED MOUNT DIABLO

Mount Diablo was sacred to the valley Native Americans, as it was to other Indian tribes who lived within sight of it. All these tribes had traditions and creation accounts that featured the mountain.

Each tribe had its name for the mountain. The Ohlone-speaking people south of Mount Diablo called it *Tuyshtak*, Northern Miwok called it *Oj.ompil.e* and Southern Miwok called it *Supremenenu*. Early Spaniards christened it *Cerro Alto de los Bolbones* (High Point of the Volvons) after the Bay Miwok Volvon tribe, which controlled the summit and eastern areas of the mountain.

The name Mount Diablo (*Devil's Thicket* translated from Spanish) originated during a Spanish expedition around 1805. The superstitious

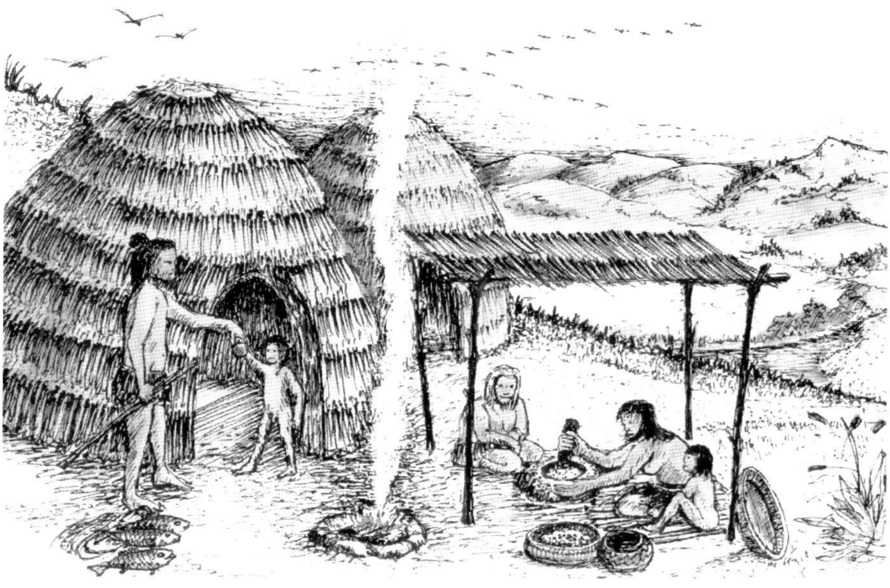

A typical East Bay–area Indian family, drawn by artist Al Greger. *Museum of the San Ramon Valley.*

Spanish soldiers called a willow thicket *Monte Diablo* when a group of Bay Miwok Indians from today's Concord escaped from them during the night. Later, the name was transferred to Mount Diablo.

THE SPANISH INVADE

In 1772, the first westerners traveled through the San Ramon Valley, led by Captain Pedro Fages. In his diary for March 31, Father Juan Crespi said that they "came to three villages with some little grass houses. As soon as the heathen caught sight of us they ran away, shouting and panic-stricken." The next day he noted that the valley had "level land, covered with grass and trees, with many and good creeks, and with numerous villages of very gentle and peaceful heathen…It is a very suitable place for a good mission."

Spanish missionaries first recorded the names by which San Ramon Indians were known to their neighbors: Seunen and Souyen. These people lived southeast of today's Norris Canyon Road in San Ramon and Dublin near various creeks.

In the fall of 1794, the Saclans (Bay Miwok from the Walnut Creek area) were the first to go to Mission Dolores in San Francisco. The Spanish weapons, their unique gifts and special music intrigued the Indians, especially the young people. Some of them wanted to ally themselves with the powerful newcomers. But, only months after they moved to Mission Dolores, an epidemic swept the mission, and in the spring of 1795, the people fled from San Francisco, returned home and resisted Spanish efforts to bring them back.

MISSION SAN JOSE

For nearly ten years beginning in the mid-1790s, the Saclans and other neighboring tribes fought against the Spanish—"gentle and peaceful" no more. Had it not been for the hostility of these tribes and the others they recruited, the Spanish would have placed Mission San Jose in the Amador, San Ramon or Diablo Valleys, instead of locating it at a site only thirteen miles from Mission Santa Clara.

Founded in 1797, this Mission attracted some Seunens beginning in 1801 as their villages began to disintegrate and the inland valleys were added

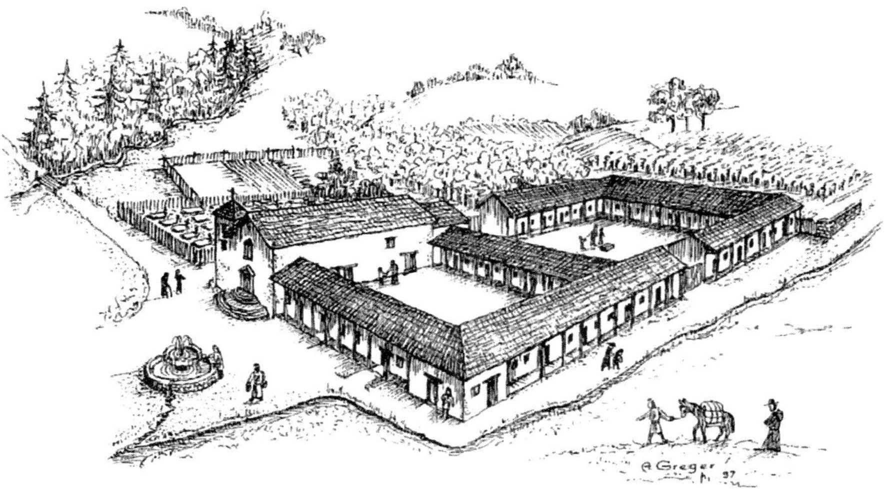

Mission San Jose as it would have looked when completed, drawn by artist Al Greger. *Museum of the San Ramon Valley.*

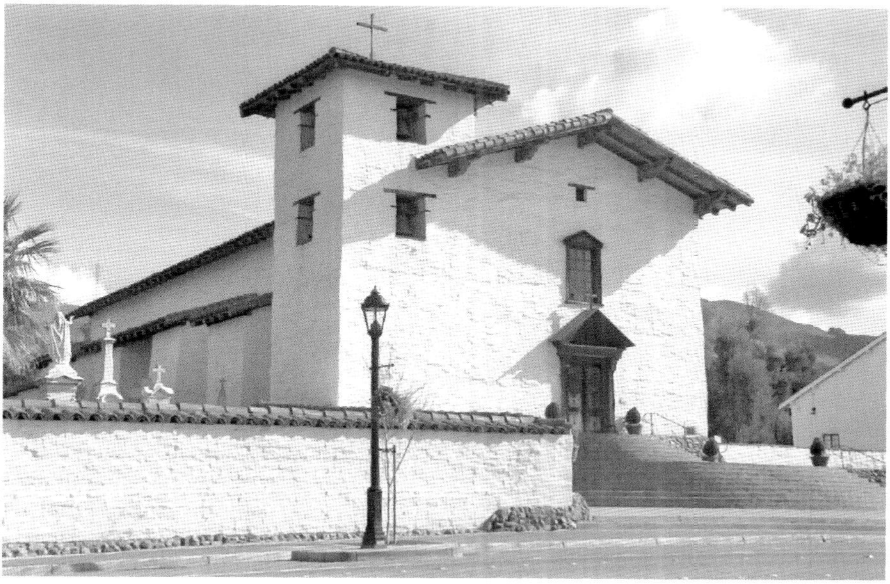

The main church at Mission San Jose was destroyed in a massive 1868 earthquake. This photograph shows the restored church, which opened in 1985. Photographer Doug Aitken. *Museum of the San Ramon Valley.*

to Mission San Jose's land. Ultimately, contact with the Spanish destroyed the Indian way of life. Livestock ravaged their carefully nurtured meadows. Western diseases and Spanish cultural and spiritual expectations altered Indian society forever.

The Rancho Era

In the 1830s, as the missions throughout California were being prepared for secularization, the pastoral rancho era began on former mission lands. Three ranchos were granted by the Mexican government in the San Ramon Valley, all using the name San Ramon.

Jose Maria Amador's Rancho San Ramon eventually included over twenty thousand acres in San Ramon with a large headquarters in today's Dublin. Mariano Castro and Bartolo Pacheco owned the northern ranchos (Danville and Alamo) and lived elsewhere because of the hostile Indian tribes around Mount Diablo. The third rancho was granted in 1843 in the Alamo–Walnut Creek area. The cattle and sheep in these ranchos were former mission livestock. Cattle hides and tallow provided the economic basis for the ranchos.

Mission San Jose became a parish church with no more temporal control over the Indians in 1836. The Indians scattered to work on the ranchos and at the Pueblo of San Jose. Some more recent recruits went back to their tribes in the Central Valley. On a rancheria in Pleasanton called Alisal, Indians from different Bay Area tribes preserved their customs and traditional religious practices for many years.

American California

When the Gold Rush began in 1848, it transformed California from a slow-paced Mexican territory into an American state. Although the Indians controlled most of the inland area, thousands of miners invaded their traditional lands and decimated these tribes. California, which entered the Union as a free state in 1850, passed laws that allowed Indians to be enslaved by any white man. Children and young women were taken and sold as servants. Not until 1863, well into the Civil War period, was the so-called Act for the Protection of the Indians repealed.

Today 723,225 American Indians live in California, with 128 in San Ramon, according to the 2010 census. Most California Indians live in urban areas, but some are still part of over one hundred established communities in their homelands.

The original Ohlone villages of San Ramon are no more. The artifacts unearthed next to creeks by bulldozers and the bedrock mortar holes on Mount Diablo remind us that a culture of great antiquity existed in this valley just 250 years ago.

Jose Maria Amador's Rancho San Ramon

One warm August night in 1834, Jose Maria Amador found himself waiting for a card game to end so he could finalize the title to his San Ramon Rancho grant. Forty-three years later, he recalled the circumstances: "The title to my rancho had been drawn up by…a secretary and amanuensis to [Governor] Figueroa, in a room at Mission San Jose…I placed [the title] in an envelope, in the hands of Señor Figueroa, requesting him to look over the documents. The Governor was playing manilla with two priests…and Eugenio Montenegro. When I voiced the request, he asked me to excuse him until he had finished playing the hand."

When the card game was over, Figueroa talked to Padre Jose Gonzalez Rubio of Mission San Jose about the title, and according to Amador, "the padre, whether willingly or not, furnished the statement as he had been ordered to do, and Figueroa then turned the documents over to me." Thus did Don Jose Maria Amador receive his formal title for the Rancho San Ramon.

Amador's life as a soldier and the owner of this rancho are well documented. In an oral history given to Thomas Savage for the Bancroft Library in 1877 and in other interviews, Amador recounted his experiences as an Indian fighter, his years as administrator of Mission San Jose, his family and his bad opinion of John Fremont and the Bear Flag revolt.

His father, Pedro, came to California with the first Spanish overland expedition in 1769. A well-respected soldier, he helped select the location for Mission San Jose and supervised construction of the first mission

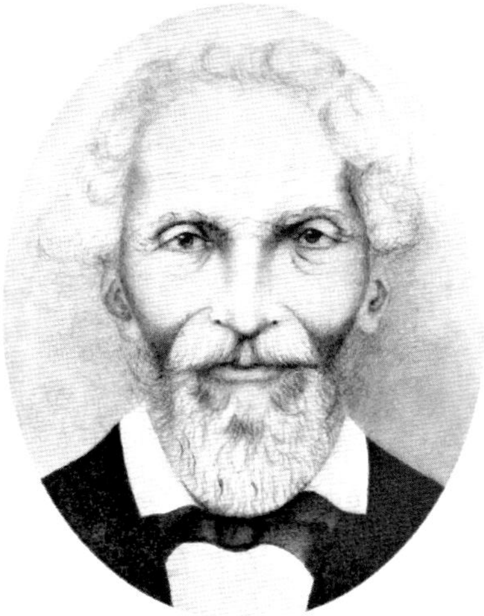

A drawing of Jose Maria Amador (1794–1883), who was granted the Rancho San Ramon for service as a soldier. *Museum of the San Ramon Valley.*

buildings in 1797. Jose Maria was born in 1794 in San Francisco. His mother, Maria Noriega Amador, was literate and taught him to read, which gave him an advantage over many others in this period.

His Rancho San Ramon grant eventually encompassed around five square leagues, or over twenty thousand acres, and covered today's San Ramon, Dougherty Valley and historic Dublin. He outlived each of his three wives. He married Maria Bernal (1802–1828) in 1818; Josepha Sanchez (1809–1838) in 1829 and Maria Soledad Alviso (b. 1829) in 1844. He later said he had twenty-seven children.

At his rancho headquarters near Alamilla Springs on today's Dublin Boulevard, he built a two-story adobe, which was occupied by James and Elizabeth Dougherty in the 1850s.

Amador stocked his land with an estimated four hundred horses, fourteen thousand cattle and three thousand sheep and planted corn, melons, vineyards and orchards. A good judge of horses, he had a number of well-trained horses on the rancho. In 1837, he and Roberto Livermore grew a successful large wheat crop in Sunol Valley, well before such crops were planted by Leo Norris and others in San Ramon.

His rancho headquarters included an adobe village for 150 workers who tended livestock and produced a wide range of leather goods (saddles, harnesses, boots, etc.), furniture and wagons. In Amador's *Recollections Concerning the History of California*, he pointed out that the Indians "were exceptional workmen."

Amador participated in the Gold Rush in the summer of 1848, just as news of the gold discovered at Sutter's Mill began to spread. He took his sons and several Indian workers and headed into today's Amador County, which was later named for him. An *Alta California* newspaper article quoted Amador as saying that he brought back three mules laden with gold, some of which was given to friends by the tin cup–full and the remainder distributed among his relatives, to be played away at *monte*.

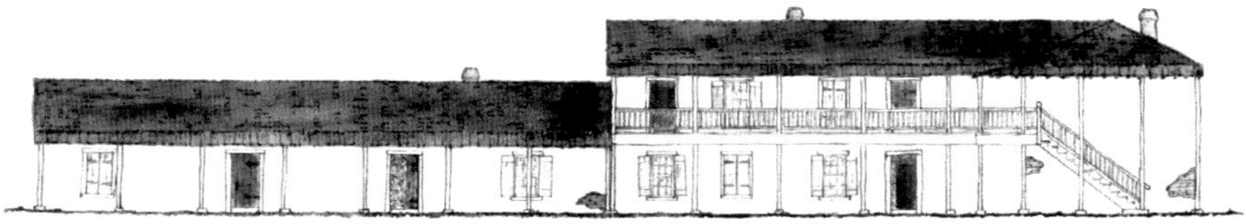

This conceptual drawing by artist John S. Hamel shows what Amador's two-story adobe probably looked like. *Museum of the San Ramon Valley.*

As Alta California moved into American hands, Amador expressed dismay at the boorish frontiersmen who imprisoned General Mariano Vallejo during the short-lived Bear Flag revolt. Soon after, Colonel John Fremont brought his California Battalion through the valley and requisitioned Amador's best tamed horses. When he asked for compensation, Fremont told Amador that "he would pay me for them with an ounce of lead from every rifle in his troop."

Finally, squatters settled on his vast rancho land, and he was unable to evict them. For this reason and needing cash, he sold his ranch to early pioneers in San Ramon and Dublin. Three of these transactions included the sale of 4,550 acres on the northwest corner to Leo and Mary Jane Norris (a deal begun in 1850), to Joel and Minerva Harlan and 10,000 acres to James Witt Dougherty and his partner William Glaskin. Today's historic Dublin area was known as "Amador" and then "Dougherty's" for decades.

Amador's long life—which bridged the Spanish, Mexican and American eras of California history—and his many recorded interviews reveal an extraordinary character. Still, he was typical of many Mexican rancho owners who were unable to make a successful transition to life in the new American state. While he ended his life in poverty and sometimes described his tale as a doleful one, in one 1875 newspaper interview he stated, "It is my wish that my reputation should be preserved and that it be said Amador wronged no man."

Early Pioneers Left Their Marks

The first San Ramon pioneers were former gold miners who purchased rancho land from Jose Maria Amador and settled down in this beautiful valley. They were part of an influx of migrants from the East who came for gold and stayed for the land. A historian in 1882 called the first valley pioneers "birds of passage" who had been to the mines, felt the blessings of the "glorious climate of California" and returned to settle. They ranched and cultivated hay and grains or were merchants who served the agricultural economy.

These names are repeated in all the early histories. They were friends who helped one another out, took meals at one another's homes, worshipped together, set up schools and shared harvest chores.

Norris

The Norris family came first. They migrated to California in 1846 and lived in Mission San Jose from 1847 to 1850. Leo and Mary Jane Norris and their children moved to San Ramon in the autumn of 1850 along with William Lynch, living in the old Soto adobe at first. Norris bought a square league (4,550 acres) in the northwest section from Jose Maria Amador that December. He and Lynch built the first frame dwelling in the valley, using redwoods from near Moraga that were hauled by way of

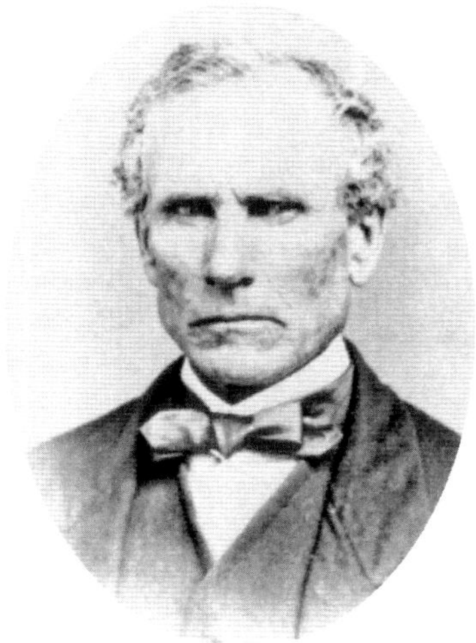

Mission San Jose and Sunol. The house lasted for a century and was destroyed by fire in 1950.

James Smith recalled Leo's son William Norris as one of the best horsemen he had ever seen, with an elegance of style and a lasso expertise few could rival. Norris probably learned his skills from Mexicans in the area since he evidently used a *riata* (leather woven rope).

A portrait of Leo Norris. He, his family and William Lynch were the first American pioneers to settle in the San Ramon Valley, arriving in the fall of 1850. *Museum of the San Ramon Valley.*

RUSSELL

In 1851, Samuel and Esther Russell and their five children moved to San Ramon. The family arrived in California in 1850 from Salt Lake and were formerly Mormons. They bought Amador rancho land just south of the Norris league, ultimately acquiring a total of 750 acres. Samuel was San Ramon's postmaster from November 20, 1852, to November 16, 1859, with the post office probably located in the Russells' home. Their ranch was just

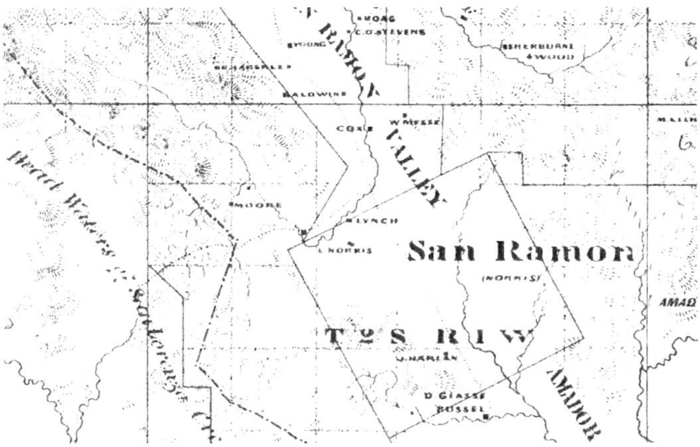

This San Ramon map in 1871 shows the locations of the Russell, Glass and Harlan ranches along the San Jose to Martinez road. *Contra Costa County Public Works.*

west of the San Jose to Martinez road, not far from David and Eliza Glass and Minerva and Joel Harlan. Today, part of the Russell property is Forest Home Farms Historic Park, where one of the barns was constructed by Russell.

HARLAN

In 1846, Minerva Fowler and Joel Harlan came to California as teenagers with his father's wagon train. They married in 1849. Joel and his cousin Jake opened a store in gold country near Coloma soon after gold was discovered. Jake wrote a book about that time called *California '46–'88*.

The Harlans bought Amador land in 1852 and built a small house, which became a landmark when Alameda County separated from Contra Costa County in 1853. One of the men marking the boundary was Joel's brother-in-law, who was familiar with the house. Joel always said they lived on the Contra Costa side.

Around 1858, the Harlans built a new Gothic Revival home on property they purchased from Norris. Called El Nido (the nest), the home became famous for its gardens and the family's hospitality and was restored in 1934.

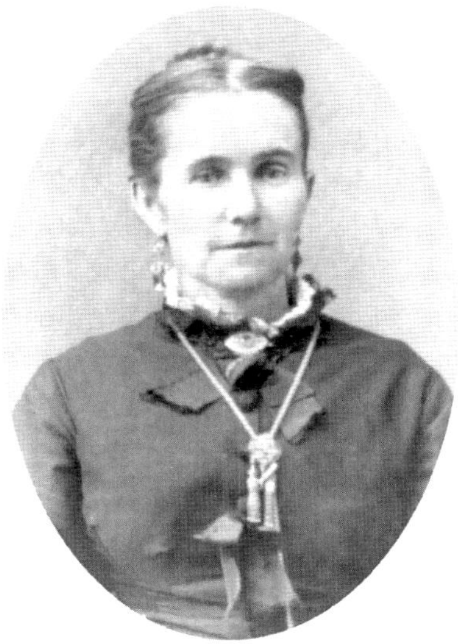
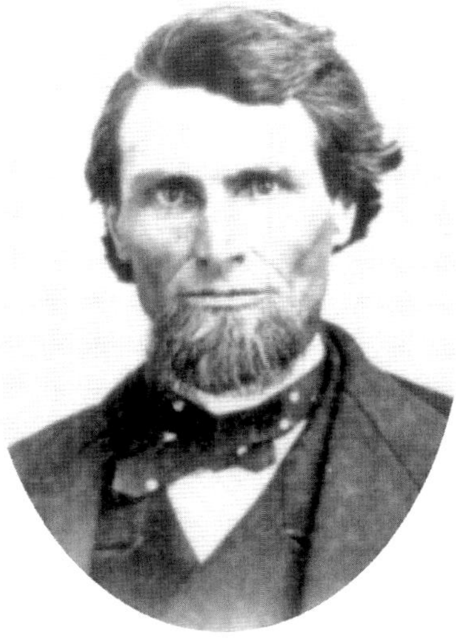

Minerva and Joel Harlan came to California in 1846 with their parents and married in 1849. They bought land from Amador and built their first house in 1852. The classic Harlan House was built farther north in 1858. *Museum of the San Ramon Valley.*

DOUGHERTY

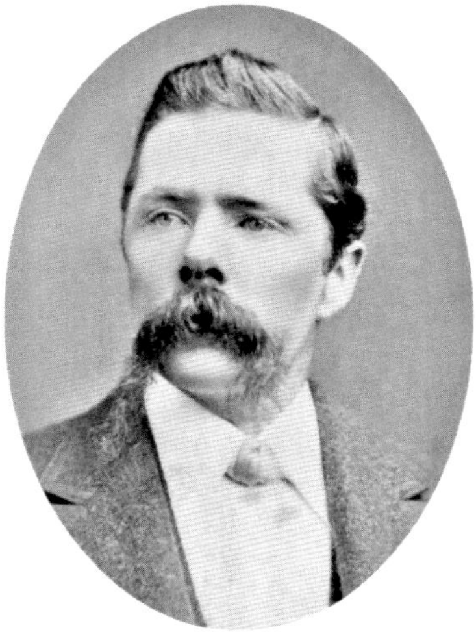

James Witt Dougherty traveled to California during the Gold Rush and set up business in Sacramento in 1849. Returning to Mississippi, he encouraged friends to come to California and brought his wife, Elizabeth, and their family to the Tri-Valley area in 1852. That year, he and a partner purchased ten thousand acres of Amador's rancho for $2,200. His family lived in Amador's large adobe (in today's Dublin) until the 1861 Calaveras earthquake demolished it.

One of the wealthiest men in Alameda County with a ranch eventually seventeen thousand acres in size, he ran thousands of cattle with the DG brand. Dougherty was elected to the Alameda County Board of Supervisors several times in the 1850s. He built an inn called Dougherty's Station in Dublin at the crossroads of two stagecoach lines.

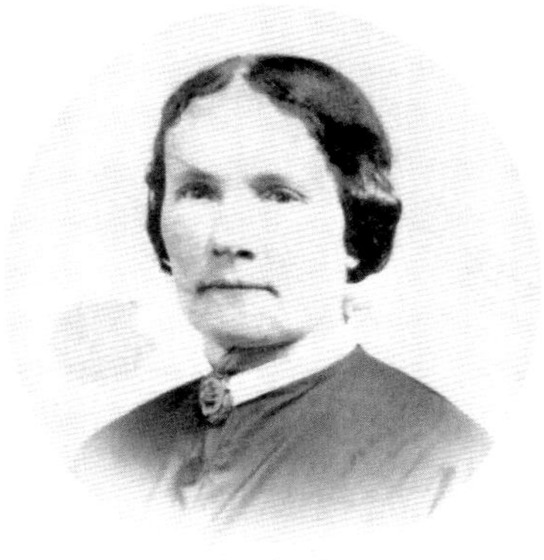

This page, top: Charles M. Dougherty, the son of James and Elizabeth Dougherty, laid out the town of Dougherty at a proposed Southern Pacific station about a mile east of Dublin. The town never materialized. *Dougherty family collection*

This page, bottom: Elizabeth Dougherty moved from Mississippi in 1852 to reunite their family in the new state of California. The Doughertys lived in Amador's two-story adobe for nearly a decade. *Dougherty family collection.*

Opposite, bottom: Pioneers gather for a picnic at Cox's Grove, circa 1890. *Left to right*: Albert W. Glass, Joe Lewis (?), Milton Larabee, William Meese, Levi Maxcy, Edward McCauley, Samuel Ramage, Lee Parker (?), Edward Shuey, Albert W. Stone, Samuel More, Charles G. Goold, John P. Chrisman, Myron W. Hall, David Glass, William Z. Stone, Nathaniel Howard, Robert O. Baldwin, James O. Boone, William Cox, George McCamley and Elisha C. Harlan. Ida Hall provided these names. *Museum of the San Ramon Valley.*

GLASS

David and Eliza Glass arrived in California early in 1850. After some merchandising in gold country, David opened a store in Alamo and planted the first apple orchard in the county. They purchased 718 acres from Norris and moved to San Ramon in 1858. The couple built a stylish Italianate home in 1877 and raised seven children there. He ranched and helped found San Ramon's Methodist Church in 1888. They were pillars of the community.

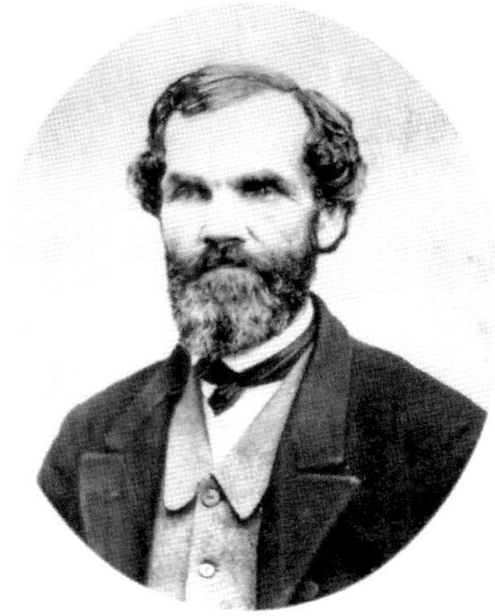

David Glass and his wife, Eliza, settled in San Ramon in 1858 after purchasing land from Leo and Mary Jane Norris along the San Jose to Martinez highway. *Museum of the San Ramon Valley.*

MCCAMLEY

George McCamley moved from the gold mines to San Ramon in 1855, purchasing a house and 375 acres of land. He and Ann Jenkinson were married in 1857. He helped bring the Danville Grange No. 85 to the valley in 1873, deeded the Southern Pacific Railroad station to the railroad subject to train use, was a school trustee and donated land for the Methodist church near their home. He left a complete farm diary dated from 1861 to 1902 that provides an invaluable look into San Ramon life of that period. His wife wrote some of the diary. Ann's niece Mary Hack married John Oswill, and their children married into the Podva and Glass families. First cousins were never far away.

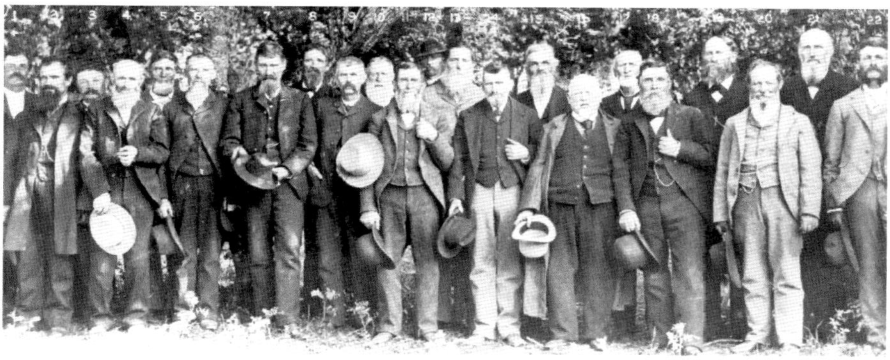

Wiedemann

Christian Wiedemann migrated from Germany in 1855 and purchased 160 acres west of the Norris league in 1867. He made a living by selling firewood and raising cattle for beef and other enterprises. He and Catherine Dittmer married in 1869, built a Gothic Revival house and had four living children.

Son Fred Wiedemann (born in 1879) was a prominent cattleman and horseman who helped found the annual Rowell Rodeos and began the locally renowned Wiedemann spring roundups and barbeques. Several generations of Wiedemann men and women were involved in all aspects of the community, including serving on school boards, cattlemen's associations, the farm bureau and fire boards. The family is still in the cattle business and active in the community today.

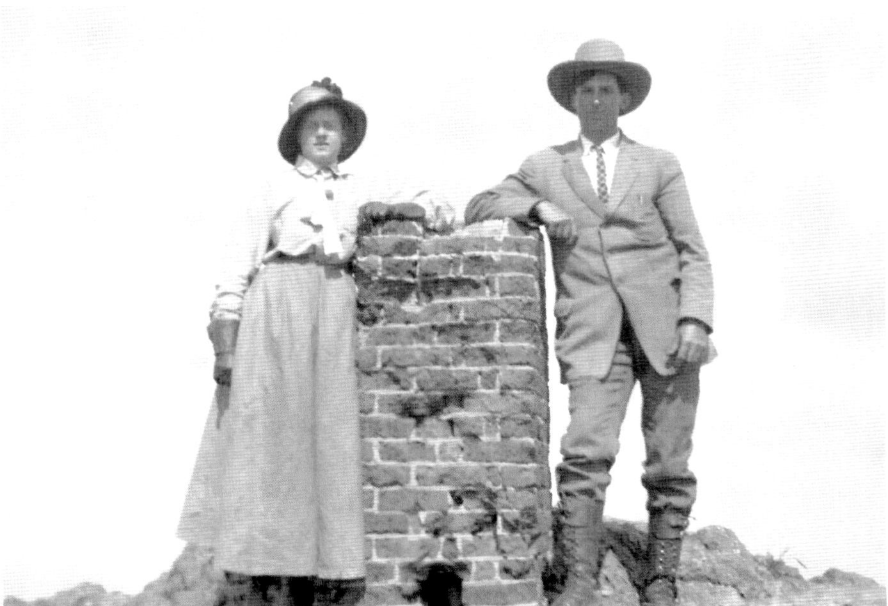

Fred and Mattie Jorgensen Wiedemann rode their horses to the "chimney" at Mount Diablo's summit. They were married in 1913. *Wiedemann family collection.*

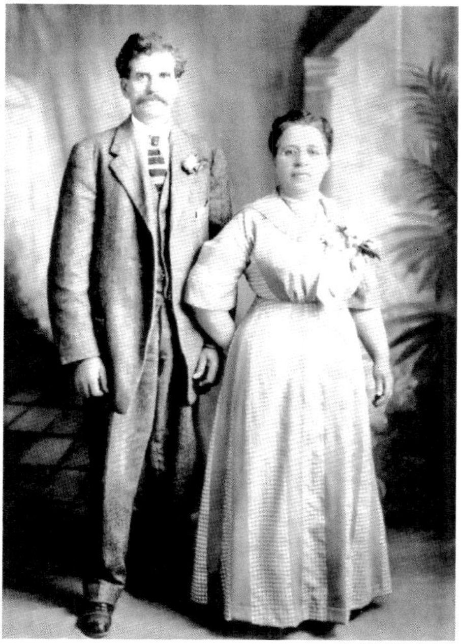

John and Delphina Fereira brought family members from Portugal to join them after 1871. They raised their fourteen children on ranches in the Dougherty Valley and Norris Canyon. *Chuck Fereira family collection.*

FEREIRA

Portuguese migrants moved into the valley early. John Fereira arrived in 1871, bringing his brother, Manuel, to San Ramon in 1878 and the rest of the family by 1883. Ambitious and strong, the Fereira brothers married, raised families and ranched in the Dougherty Valley until they got their stake. About 1900, John and wife Delphina (eventually with fourteen children) bought a ranch just south of Norris Canyon Road. Manuel, wife Leonora and their four children moved to a ranch in Bollinger Canyon, not far north of Crow Canyon Road.

Manuel and Leonora's son William Carlos Fereira bought the San Ramon General Store in 1924 and was postmaster for over thirty years. The store was the heart of the village, a gathering place for everyone. Their grandson Bill helped found the San Ramon Fire District in 1963 and was the first chief.

San Ramon Could Have Been Limerick

The name "San Ramon" is the oldest in the San Ramon Valley. Nevertheless, it took several decades before it was firmly fixed to the historic village. The area had several other names beginning in the 1850s.

The village was first known as "Brewensville" after Levi Brewen, the first blacksmith to set up shop in San Ramon. Frequently, places were named for a person whose shop or skill was important to the area, and the blacksmith's trade was essential to early ranchers and farmers.

The next name was "Lynchville" for William Lynch, an energetic early pioneer who came to the valley in 1850 as a young man, helped Leo Norris build the first two-story frame house in San Ramon and married Leo's daughter Mary Norris. He was prominent in the valley for many years as a carpenter, rancher and self-taught doctor. They had the first American child born in San Ramon (1853), Leo Lynch. Leo opened a merchandise store, was a rancher and served as San Ramon's postmaster from 1876 to 1883.

"Limerick" then appeared on the map when settlers from Ireland began to move in, bringing with them familiar names from home. As the Irish famines of the 1840s devastated that country, visionaries in England and Ireland promoted California as a haven for migrants.

In 1845, one Irish priest, Eugene McNamara, petitioned the Mexican government asking for land in California. He wanted to bring two thousand Irish Catholic families "as a barrier against invading 'Methodist wolves' of the United States," according to Kevin Starr in *Americans and the California Dream*.

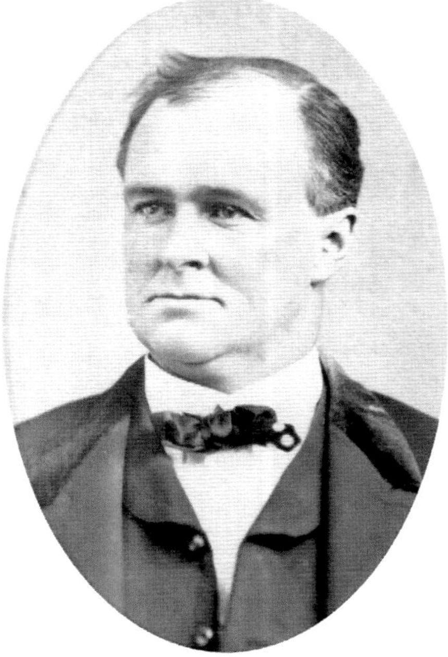
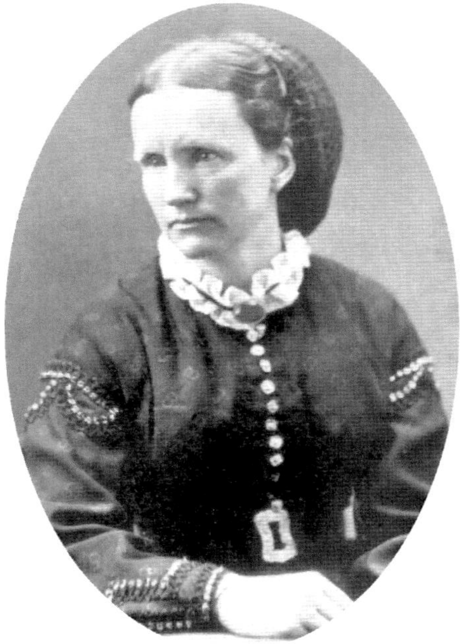

William Lynch and Marry Norris arrived in San Ramon in 1850 with her parents and were married in 1852. The community was briefly named Lynchville after this active and neighborly man. *Museum of the San Ramon Valley.*

While that petition was unsuccessful, the idea of available land in California stayed with many European migrants of that period. By the 1860 census, 20.4 percent of the foreign-born settlers in Contra Costa's Township Two were Irish. Most of the Amador rancho covered San Ramon and had been purchased by James W. Dougherty, whose father was an Irish immigrant.

The name "San Ramon" had been around for a long time, beginning at least in the 1820s. The creek coming from Bollinger Canyon became San Ramon Creek as it curved north through the young village. Before 1848, three Mexican ranchos in the valley also carried the name: Rancho San Ramon (Amador), Rancho San Ramon (Castro/Pacheco) and, to the north, El Sobrante de San Ramon (Romero).

Jose Maria Amador, the owner of Rancho San Ramon, testified in an 1855 land case about the name's origin: "The name was given it [the creek] by a mayor domo [of Mission San Jose] by the name of Ramon who had the care of some sheep there a long time ago." He said that "San" was added

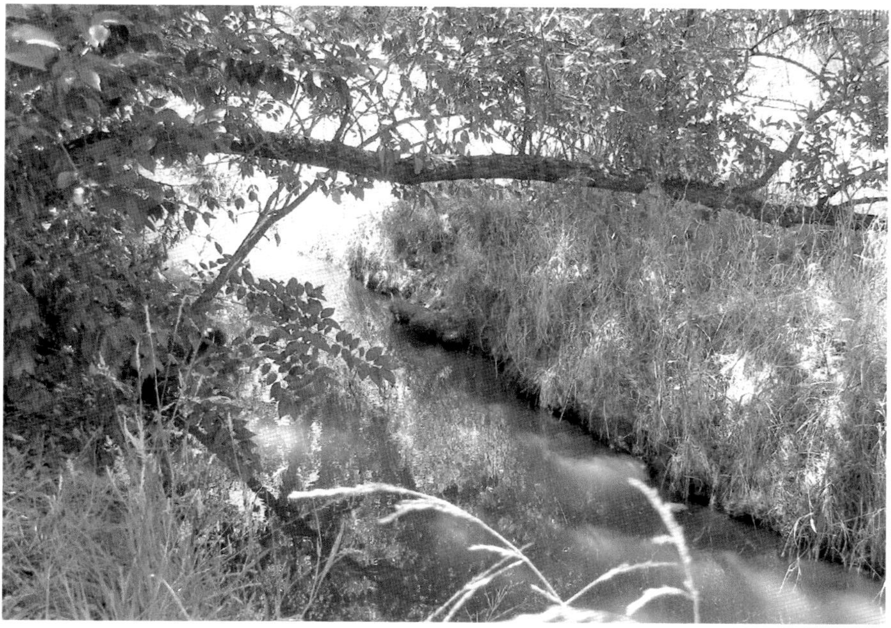

San Ramon Creek and its fifty-four-square mile watershed cover the northern part of the San Ramon Valley. *Museum of the San Ramon Valley.*

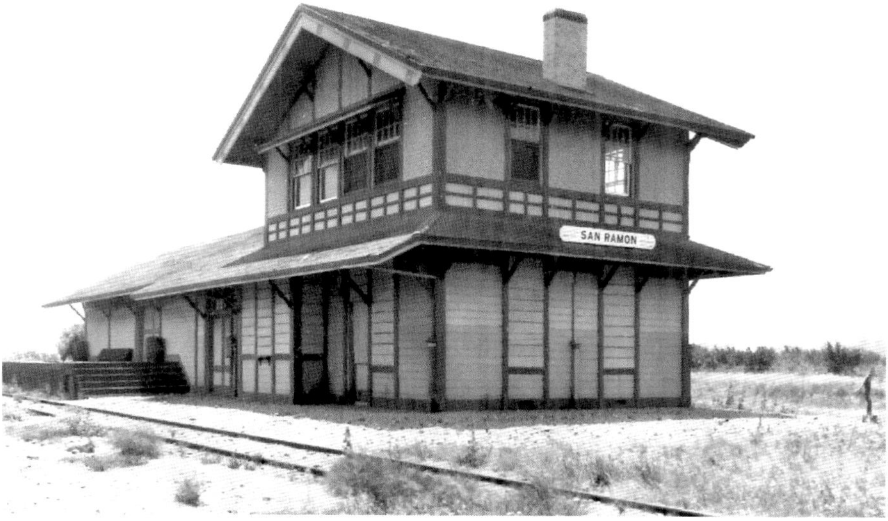

San Ramon's two-story combination depot was identical to those in Concord, Walnut Creek and Danville. The large station also included an engine house and a turnaround. *Museum of the San Ramon Valley.*

to Ramon's name to conform to the usual way Spanish names appeared. Ramon was the name given to him when he was baptized at the mission.

A San Ramon post office with Samuel Russell as postmaster was in place from 1852 to 1859; it was reestablished on December 4, 1873. In 1882, historian J.P. Munro-Fraser wrote that the name "San Ramon" was the one "given to the Post-office at what is usually known as the village of Limerick." Howard Fereira recalled old-timers calling the land south of San Ramon Creek "Limerick" and the area north of the creek "San Ramon."

Only when the railroad arrived in 1891 was the name San Ramon established for good. From 1891 to 1907, San Ramon was the terminus of Southern Pacific's San Ramon Branch Line, although the village itself was half a mile away from the railroad station.

Today, San Ramon is a thriving city and can proudly claim one of the oldest city names in California. Two Dougherty Valley parks commemorate these early names: Limerick and Rancho San Ramon Community Park.

Farmers and Ranchers of San Ramon

Writers who first described San Ramon and the adjacent inland valleys had nothing but praise for the soil and the weather. A special *Contra Costa Gazette* newspaper edition in 1912 described one San Ramon Valley ranch that produced peaches, prunes, hay and grapes as "typical of the unlimited capacity of this section of our county for all agricultural, viticultural and horticultural growths."

R.O. Baldwin farmed just north of San Ramon and called the valley a Garden of Eden.

Ohlone Indians, who lived here successfully for eons, made use of diverse natural resources. They burned meadows regularly to produce desirable grasses and seeds and cultivated various bulbs. In the late eighteenth century, Spanish missionaries introduced cattle and sheep and brought new plants that rapidly changed the landscape of Alta California, including nonnative grasses such as wild oats. The Mexican rancheros grazed livestock and usually planted small gardens for domestic use.

For a century after California statehood in 1850, people in San Ramon made their living from agriculture. They grazed livestock; raised grains, hay, grapes and tomatoes; and planted fruit and nut orchards. San Ramon's first American settler, Leo Norris, planted wheat, which reportedly produced an astonishing 110 bushels to the acre in 1851.

San Ramon's mild, Mediterranean weather with rainy winters was unusual to the new settlers, but they soon learned which crops benefited from this weather pattern. They started dry farming, relying on water from

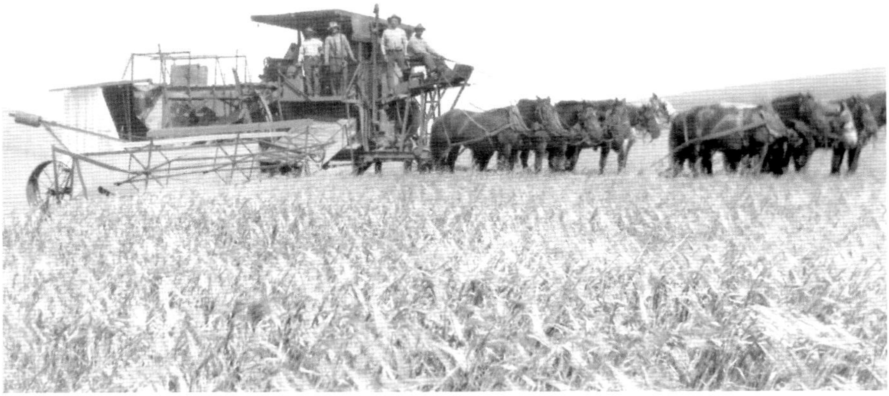

Plenty of horsepower was needed to pull the Wiedemanns' gasoline-powered combined harvester. It was used in fields throughout the San Ramon Valley to reap grain during the '20s and '30s. *Wiedemann family collection.*

winter rains, springs and creeks. The Bishop Ranch had an aquifer, which allowed them to dig wells and irrigate their orchards, the only irrigation in the valley. All these enterprises were affected by the weather, availability of water, changing technology and evolving markets.

The industrial revolution changed farming methods over the years, from the early practice of harvest by hand using scythes, to horse-powered machines, then stationary threshing machines and finally to combines able to cut and thresh while moving through the fields. Steam engines and teams of as many as twenty workhorses provided power for the work. Gasoline-powered tractors began to take over much of the heavy flat land work in the early twentieth century while tractors capable of working hillsides arrived in the 1930s. Horses were used for light jobs, such as hay work, through World War II.

Initially, wheat was the major cash crop for the Contra Costa farmers. It was a hard, dry variety that shipped well and made good bread. Transported from wharves at Pacheco and Martinez or Roberts Landing on the bay below San Leandro, the county's grain brought premium prices at the Liverpool, England Corn Exchange.

For their own use, farmers had wheat ground into flour at the Pacheco Flour Mill, a long day's drive on dusty and sometimes muddy roads. When the Southern Pacific came to the valley in 1891, this long haul was eliminated.

When Christian and Catherine Wiedemann settled in the western hills in the 1860s, they made a living selling firewood, cultivating apples and hay, raising cattle and horses and selling meat. He purchased the Povis brand, PS (first registered in 1856). The Wiedemanns continue to use the PS on their cattle, making it probably the oldest brand in continuous use in California.

Leo Norris, his son-in-law William Lynch, David Glass, Joel and Minerva Harlan, George McCamley and others grazed cattle, cultivated wheat and grew hay. As wheat prices fell, they added almonds, fruit trees (prunes, pears, cherry, apple), tomatoes and walnuts. There were some dairies that bought cream from the ranches. Many of these products went to canneries in Walnut Creek and Hayward. Diversified farming was their approach, anything that would make a living.

"Hay, from volunteer grasses or planted grain, was of almost equal importance as wheat. San Francisco was the major market for hay because of its liveries, the cavalry at the Presidio and the many draft horses which supported docks and commerce. Scows, loaded with locally grown hay, plied the bay from docks in Pacheco, Martinez and Hayward to the special hay wharf in San Francisco," according to Ralph Cozine.

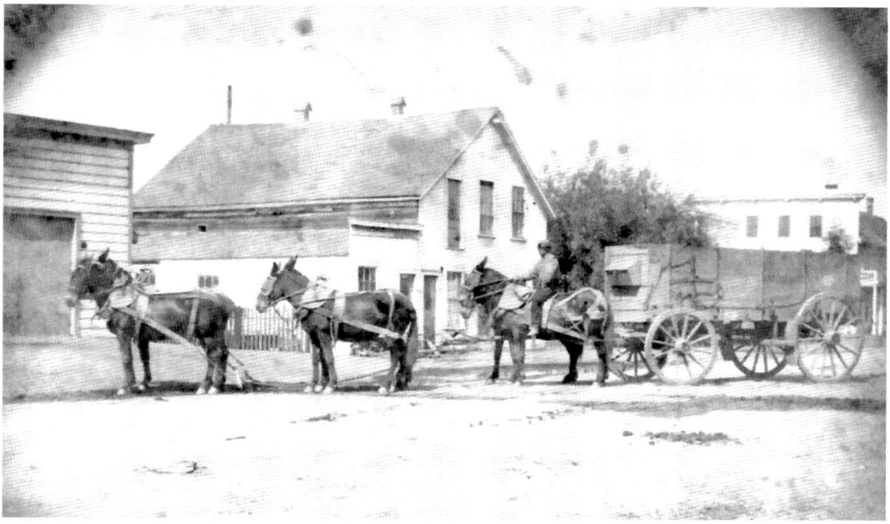

This Norris wagon, shown in 1868 at San Ramon Village, is loaded with sacks of grain pulled by a six-horse team. It could be on its way to Pacheco or Roberts Landing near San Leandro. *Museum of the San Ramon Valley.*

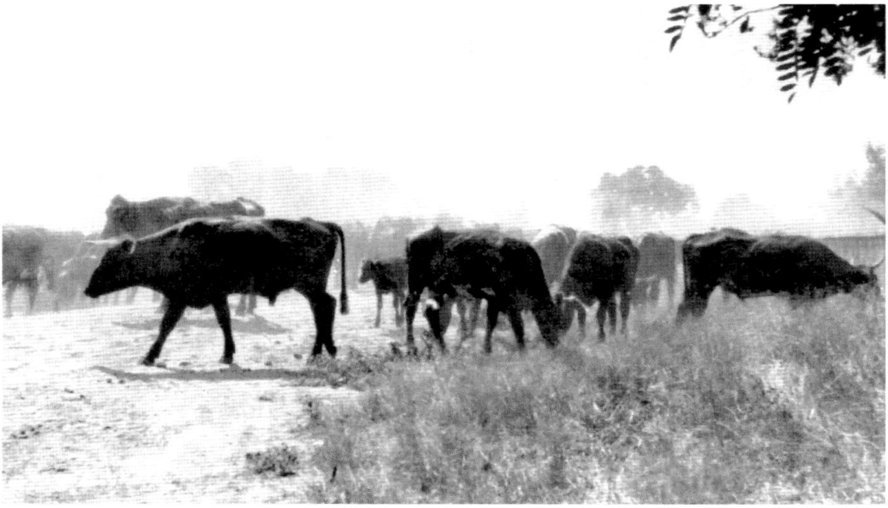

Cattle on the Glass Ranch are shown in the hills above San Ramon. Anita and Loretta Glass ran the ranch for thirty years in the twentieth century, calling it Lora Nita Ranch. *Museum of the San Ramon Valley.*

In an interview, Rudy Banke described the usual Dougherty Valley ranch practices: "We planted wheat and barley along the flats and on the hills that weren't too steep. The first year we'd sow wheat or barley; the second year that same field would be in volunteer hay; and the third year it was pasture for the cattle…In the spring we'd use a team of seven horses to run a cultivator over the field where we'd want to grow grain, so as to break up the adobe soil."

Alamo's Myron Hall grafted a Persian (also called English) walnut onto a native black walnut tree in 1873, producing an easily cracked, flavorful nut. Scions from that tree were used in many of the earliest local walnut orchards. Hall and Frank Rutherford at the Bishop Brothers Ranch were leaders in walnut culture, as hundreds of acres of these walnuts were planted in the inland valleys. Walnuts became the major cash crop. New orchards were still being planted after World War II. In Walnut Creek, growers established the Contra Costa Walnut Growers Association, which graded, packaged and sold most of the county's production.

Travis Boone of Forest Home Farms provided custom harvesting, hulling and drying services for ranches throughout the area well into the 1960s. He invented and marketed towers that were used throughout the state for knocking walnuts, picking prunes, pruning and spraying. Several of the large

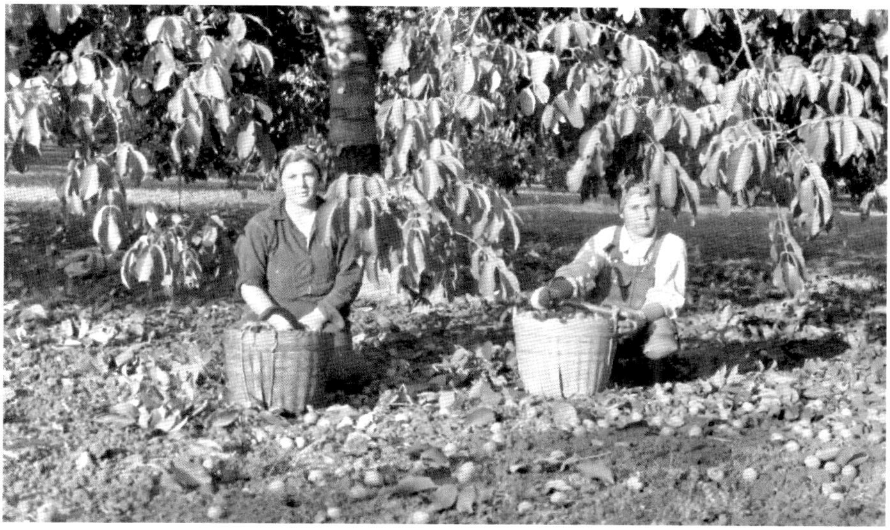

Above: These women are picking walnuts and placing them in bags on Boone Ranch. Ruth Boone managed a "women's crew" for years, although she never thought she would do anything like that. *Museum of the San Ramon Valley.*

Below: This Bishop Ranch lithograph advertises California Bartlett Pears. Bishop Ranch shipped pears to the East Coast using boxes with these colorful pictures. *Museum of the San Ramon Valley.*

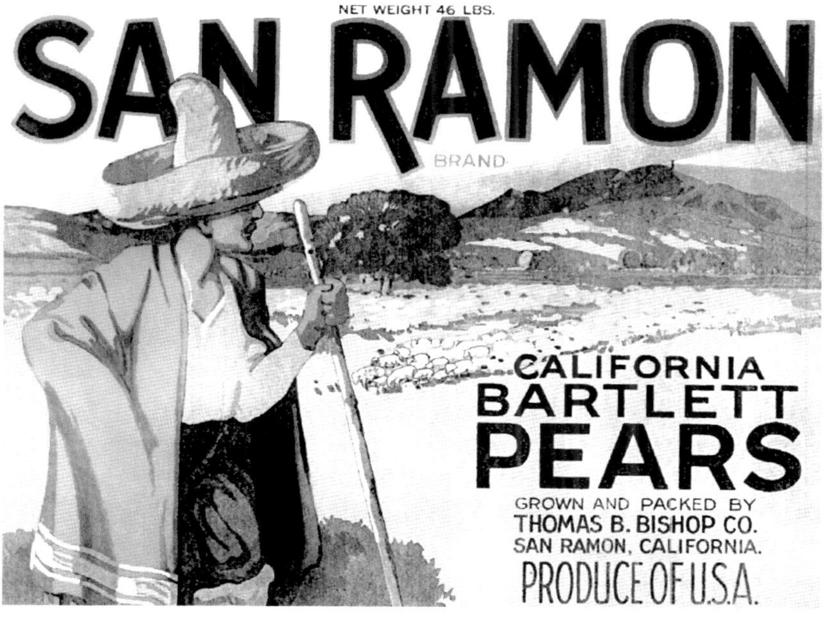

local ranches had their own hulling and drying equipment. During World War II, San Ramon Valley High School closed for the walnut harvest so that students could pick and sack walnuts for transport to the hullers. Stains on their hands from the walnut hulls took weeks to wear off.

Pears were planted on the Bishop Ranch by Rutherford in 1911, eventually on three hundred irrigated acres. The ranch's Bartletts were shipped directly from its railroad siding, and San Ramon's pears were well known in East Coast markets. Smaller pears went to local canneries in Hayward and Walnut Creek.

The Bishop Ranch had an airstrip from which Don Price flew a Stearman airplane to dust and spray orchards from 1946 to the late '50s. At different seasons, he applied dusts and sprays to the orchards and sprayed the grain crops with 24D, which killed mustard and other broadleaf weeds. He flew in the morning when there was no wind. He made plenty of noise.

Most of the agriculture in the valley came to an end with suburban development in the 1960s. While San Ramon families such as the Wiedemanns and Henrys would have preferred to continue ranching, agriculture became unviable. Increased taxes forced them out as their land was taxed at market rates (housing), ranches were included in assessment districts for modern infrastructure and inheritance taxes harmed many of them. The owners of Baldwin Ranch, just north of San Ramon, saw their annual tax bill rise from $4,000 to $40,000, leaving no choice but to sell to housing developers.

In addition to tax impacts, new residents arrived who objected to aerial crop dusting and let their dogs loose to chase the livestock. Vandals damaged tractors, cut fences and did wheelies on ranch lands. Although the new folks said that they valued the open space and clear air, many of them did not acknowledge that the agricultural lands surrounding them were private property.

In the early '60s, the Wiedemann family was probably the largest tax payer in the county. They grazed (on their own and leased land) over eight thousand acres in San Ramon. When the Bishop Ranch was planned as a "new town" in the early '70s, a huge assessment district was established by the county, which was applied to some of the Wiedemann ranch land around Alcosta Boulevard, to devastating effect.

In another sign of "progress," Ruth Boone of Forest Home Farms said that Pacific Gas and Electric bought a swath of their property for transmission lines and a power plant, presenting them with an ultimatum and a price for the land, which they eventually took. She said, "They forced us to sell the land."

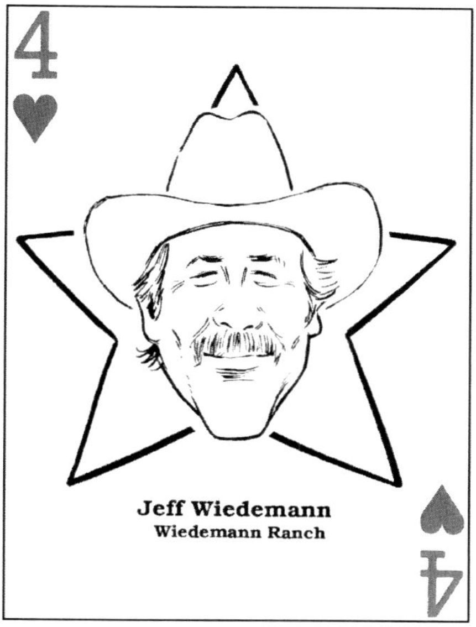

Rancher Jeff Wiedemann on a playing card, drawn in 1988. *Museum of the San Ramon Valley.*

A.W. Henry tried to continue raising his Black Angus cattle and initially refused to sell his valley land to developers Ken Volk and Bob McLain. When the two men bought property north and south of Henry's Diamond Welford Ranch and threatened to include the Henry spread inside the assessment district, he reluctantly sold the ranch.

The Wiedemanns continue to graze cattle in San Ramon and Tassajara. Jeff Wiedemann was clear about the demise of agriculture in San Ramon, stating in a *San Ramon Valley Times* article, "The only reason there are houses in the San Ramon Valley is that ranchers got squeezed out." His aunt Ann Wiedemann Kaplan tried to make the best of these changes and was quoted in the newspaper as saying, "It's too bad that it is all being developed, but what can you do? It is a beautiful area with wonderful climate and you can't fault people for wanting to live here."

San Ramon Scholars

San Ramon pioneers started schools for their children very early, building the first schoolhouse in the valley. The 1882 county history states that an early San Ramon school was constructed in 1852 at the "foot of the eminence which is known as Cox's hill, near the village of Limerick [San Ramon]." James Smith wrote that several local families (probably Norris, Glass, Harlan and Russell) contributed labor and material for its erection and hauled the lumber from the redwoods west of Moraga Valley.

Other early San Ramon schools are mentioned: one near a clump of oaks on Leo Norris's land was taught by Sylvester Degan. In 1856 or 1857, another school stood near the Glass store in San Ramon. Smith tutored the Harlan and Glass children in their homes for a season as well.

After a failed school bond election in 1864, voters supported a tax of $2,000 to purchase land and erect a new schoolhouse on October 27, 1866. The San Ramon Grammar School was constructed in 1867 and served the community for over eighty years. Carpenter Ebenizer Dole built the all-wood and fondly remembered building, which measured forty-six by twenty-six feet in dimensions, had a thirteen-foot-high ceiling and featured an impressive bell tower. There were two rooms: grades one to four used the smaller room, and grades five to eight occupied the larger.

"The building is one among the neatest and best arranged school houses in the county," according to a writer for the *Contra Costa Gazette* in 1874.

James Smith recalled a teacher from Stockton in the 1850s named Miss Everett, who would read a chapter from the Bible and pray. She had

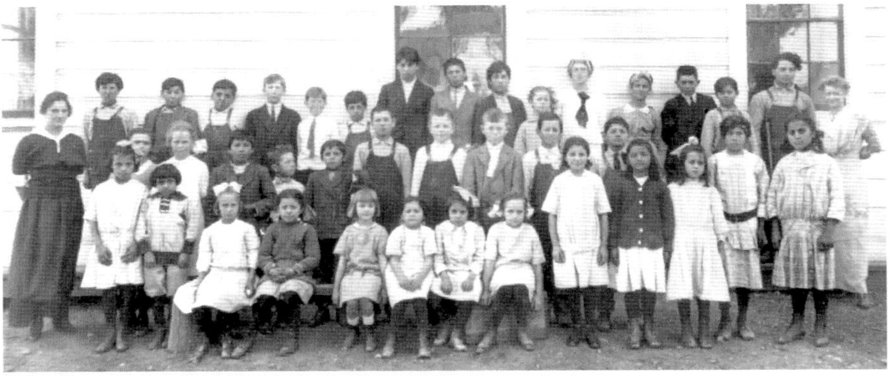

San Ramon Grammar School students in 1914 with teachers Ella Boucher (far left) and Blanch Wilson (far right). *Students from left to right, first row*: Rose Peters, Less Thomas, Petrea Thorup, Mary Souves, Thelma Oswill, Varonica Cabral, Evelyn Peters, Vita Jensen; *second row*: Helen Read, Dorothy Wilcox, Josh Souves, Loury Loston, Tony Souves, Antonio Santas, Simson Johnson, Ken Fry, Tony Fernandos, Polly Fereira, Tony Gonzalves, E. Gonsalves, Leonora Santas, Mary Mattos, Amelie Santos; *third row*: Joe Mattos, ? Souves, Bert Peters, Ed Olsson, Rowland Glass, Ed Peters, Ambrose Swartz, M. Santas, Manuel Mattos, Eleanor Boone, Ramona Read, Christ Sorenson, Travis Boone, Joe Rosaf, Ed Fereira. *Museum of the San Ramon Valley.*

some problems with the older boys and "would shed tears because of their conduct." Albert J. Young taught at the new school from 1867 to 1869 and 1873 to 1877. A rather severe man, there were no reports of discipline problems when he was in charge.

In 1874, the trustees were William Cox, George McCamley and Mrs. James O. Boone. The boundary between the Danville and San Ramon Grammar School districts was established between the Baldwin and Meese Ranches in 1880, with the Cox ranch just south of Meese's spread. Meese's property is today's Greenbrook Homes.

During the 1890s, enrollment hovered around 110 students. In 1896, the school grounds were beautified by the San Ramon Public Hall Association. These improvements included a new fence and stile on the south side, rustic seats throughout the grounds, an awning for the girls' yard and a ring and bars for the boys' area.

William H. Langdon was the best known of any San Ramon School graduate. A brilliant student, he became an educator, attorney, banker and judge. He was the city attorney of San Francisco, a candidate for California Governor in 1906 and, from 1927 to 1939, a California Supreme Court judge.

The San Ramon School also served as a social center for the community since it was the only large local space available for fifty years. Henry Wiedemann and Leo Lynch remembered removing the school's central partition for graduations and other events. The building was used to hold May Day festivities, flag ceremonies, spelling bees, meetings, graduations and parties.

Many of these farm kids stopped formal education when they graduated from grammar school. A few attended high school, boarding in Oakland or San Francisco. In 1910, Grange members organized a local public high school, which first met in a converted house on Church Street in Danville. Viola Lynch recalled picking up fellow students in a horse and buggy to

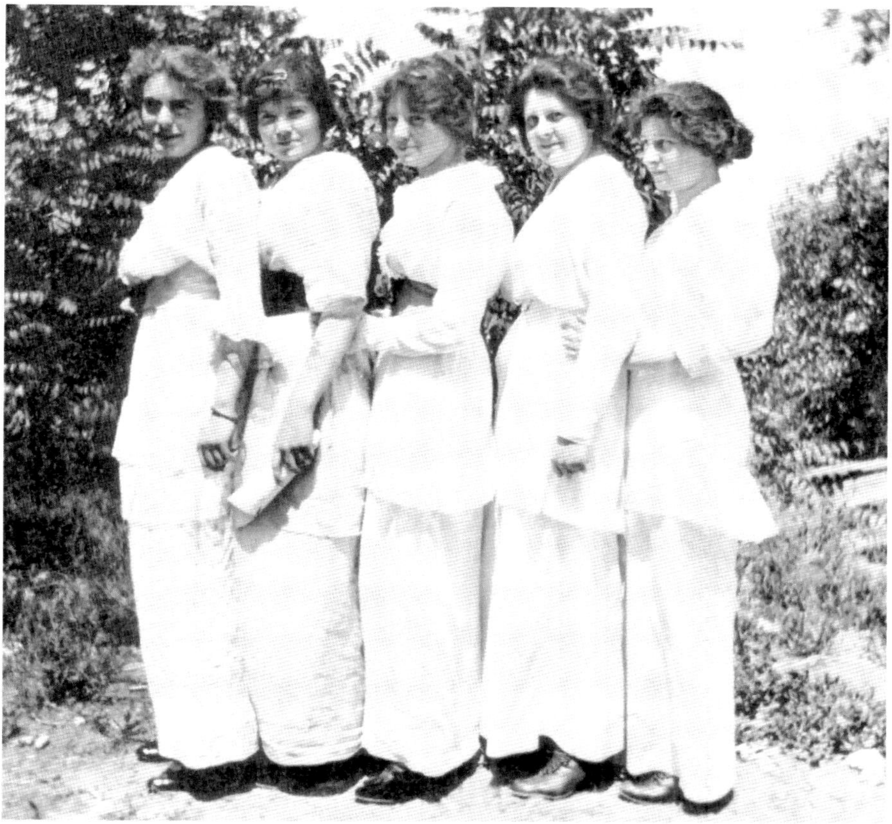

The first four-year graduates of San Ramon Valley High School in 1914 are, *left to right*: Astrid Olsson, Ora Bell, Ruth Weinhauser, Viola Lynch and Alice Bell. *Museum of the San Ramon Valley.*

travel north to high school along the old highway. In 1914, the San Ramon Valley Union High School graduated its first class, which included San Ramon's Viola Lynch and Astrid Olsson.

In 1922, the Danville Union Elementary School District was created, and a modern four-room elementary school was built. The San Ramon trustees discussed joining that district but decided against it. In 1945, farmer-educator Roger Schulte and rancher Fred Wiedemann debated the issue again, but the trustees retained their original district. San Ramon kept its own grammar school district until 1965, when all valley high school and grammar school districts unified.

During the '30s, when good news was needed by everyone, several outstanding high school athletes won top awards at state track meets, and the football team had victorious seasons, remarkable for such a small school. Howard Fereira believed the San Ramon Grammar School track team might have existed for only one year, 1932.

In June 1933, Lee Fereira won the Junior Pentathalon in Berkeley over seventy-eight other competitors. This competition, started that year by the *Oakland Tribune*, featured basketball efficiency, the seventy-five-yard dash, ball put (shot put), broad jump and high jump. His winning points for the meet were 4,409, the fourth best in the world that year.

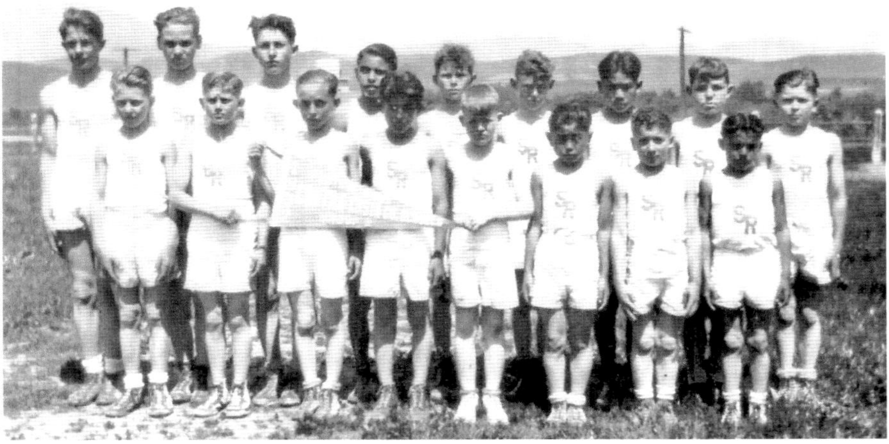

San Ramon School track team in 1932, arranged by age and height. *Left to right, back row*: Lee Fereira, unknown, Norman Amarant, Elmer Soto, unknown, unknown, unknown, Mike Conners, Bill Fereira; *front row*: Roger Hawley, Lorenzo Oreglia, Ed Amarant, unknown, George Steinmetz, unknown, Cliff Fereira, Bill Soto.

However, 1935 was the year valley residents remember best for their high school teams. Lee Fereira (who was also the quarterback) said, "We were fortunate then because we had a lot of really good athletes, all around the same time. Heck, our starting backfield in football was also our relay team…When we had a home [football] game on Friday afternoons, everyone closed up their business to come and watch us play." The small high school had a perfect football season, 8-0.

With the old grammar school "termite- and dry rot–ridden," according to teacher Irene Schulte, a new three-room elementary school was built in 1949 and opened in 1950 south of the village. There were not enough students to fill all the rooms, so the middle room was saved for other uses like music class for the whole school. Jeff Wiedemann recalled there were six students in his class in the '60s.

According to Sandee Wiedemann, "An annual event was to close the school for the day and everyone would bring their lunch and walk across the field to our house to swim in the pool that Dad built in 1950. Pools were rare in San Ramon then and this was a pretty big deal."

Today, a plaque from the San Ramon Valley Historical Society on San Ramon Valley Boulevard north of Deerwood Road marks the location of the original San Ramon Grammar School, which was razed in 1960. It is gone, but definitely not forgotten.

After the Civil War in San Ramon

San Ramon in the 1860s and 1870s became a lively little village located at the intersection of the old highway, the road to Crow Canyon and the bridge over San Ramon Creek.

People often think the Civil War did not concern Californians—quite the opposite. When the war started in 1860, opinions ran high about the South's right to secede versus Abraham Lincoln's call for the Union. Many early settlers had migrated from border states back east. In fact, in the presidential election of 1864, San Ramon and Danville voters supported George McClellan over Lincoln, ninety-one to seventy-six.

Several well-known San Ramon folks were outspoken in their support for the Union. They included E.H. Cox, David Glass and the Crow brothers. Family lore says that, after Lincoln was elected in 1860, Glass left the Democratic Party and became a Republican, setting the party affiliation for Glass descendants from then on.

San Ramon–area Democrats included William Norris, Albert G. Wilkes, Dan and Andrew Inman, Felix Coats, Golder Field, Van Hayes, Edward Sturgeon and Jesse Bowles. Both Wilkes and Andrew Inman had a black servant in their home, according to the 1860 census.

One July 4 celebration in 1864 reflected the tensions in the valley. A recitation of the Declaration of Independence was interpreted by the Crow brothers to be sympathetic to the Southern cause. According to a report by James Smith, "One of the Crow family arose and in forceful language asserted, 'No secession speech shall be delivered here,' and followed with

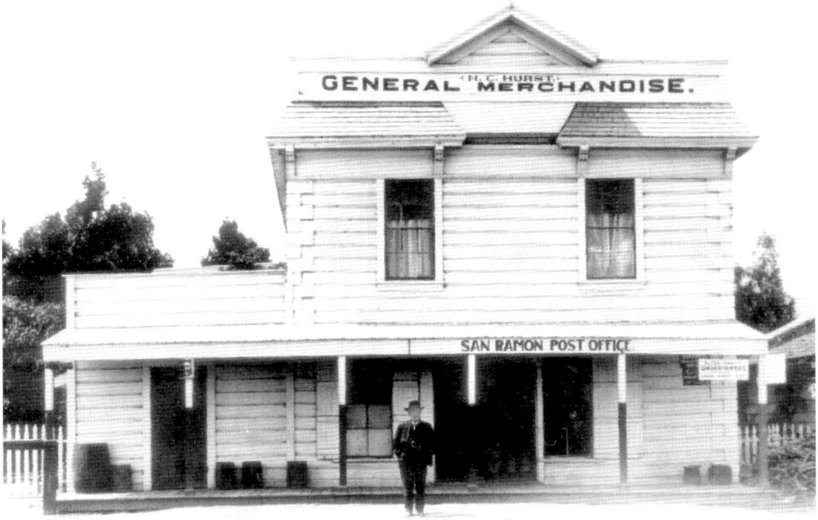

The general store and San Ramon post office shows Henry Hurst standing in front, in 1911. *Museum of the San Ramon Valley.*

more strong language. All the Crows flocked together and for a short time there was great excitement that resulted in the meeting being broken up."

San Ramon's general stores would have been likely places for debates over the Civil War and other topics. In the 1860s, the village had several stores, a blacksmith shop and a hotel.

The general merchandise store offered supplies and housed the post office. In its early years, it was owned by Frank Glass, C.C. Lewelling, Henry Hurst, his son Harry Hurst and then William C. Fereira, according to Henry Wiedemann. The store was San Ramon's stagecoach stop from 1864 to 1891. People hanging around would watch for the puff of road dust signaling the stagecoach coming south over Peter's hill. Hurst's San Ramon store had an open-door policy in which patrons wrote down their purchases if no one was around.

The *Contra Costa Gazette* depicts San Ramon on July 18, 1868:

> *San Ramon*
>
> *On entering San Ramon* [familiarly known as "Limerick"] *the first pleasing feature is the public school house, said to be the finest in the country.*

It shows that the people are not only tasty, but that they have a liberal spirit, and believe that what is worth doing is worth doing well. Miss Jennie E. Dowling has a fine school there of 43 pupils in average attendance.

The Good Templars have a lively organization, and the Sabbath school is well attended. Mr. Brewen was hard at work in his blacksmith shop, and the wheelwrights had enough business to encourage them to erect two nice cottages for their families. There is a store in the place, and also a public hotel.

The village is on the high land in the valley, the water on either side flowing in opposite directions. The place must be nearly 1,000 feet above the level of the sea, and is subject to severe winds and sudden changes in the atmosphere.

Continuing the road, we find extra crops of grain and some fine buildings. Mr. Joel Harlan has a large ranch, the grain land being cultivated on shares by Mr. Bennett for this year. By an upright course he [Harlan] *has acquired quite a little fortune, and this we find him enjoying in a quiet unassuming way. He has good farm buildings and an extra stock of horses. He has recently purchased a "section" of land in the San Joaquin valley, and intends farming two ranches next year. Mr. Glass, adjoining, is doing quite an amount of farming on his extensive ranch.*

The *Contra Costa Gazette* reports on July Fourth on July 15, 1871:

The Fourth at Limerick

The manner in which a people celebrate their local holidays is a fair criterion by which to determine at once their patriotism and their refinement. In the United States, "the day we celebrate" is the 4th of July.

It was the good fortune of the writer to be present at some exercises given by the pupils of San Ramon School on the 4th. At 10:30 A.M., several hundred persons being assembled in the school room [for] *appropriate songs and declamations followed.*

It was universally admitted that all who participated in the exercises had acquitted themselves well. So brief time had been devoted to preparation that fears were entertained for the success of some, but happily there were no failures to record. In fact all did so well, that it is scarcely just to particularize any pieces as superior to others; but was not the delivery of the "Supposed Speech of John Adams" by Miss Ida Meese, and the reading of the "Declaration" by Miss Mary Lynch especially deserving of commendation? The "American Flag," a poem with response to each stanza was delivered in excellent style by the 3d Reader Class. The stanzas were repeated by a little girl, who held in her hand the flag to which her poem referred, the American flag. The response was uttered in united voice by several boys and girls.

At 12 M., all present repaired to a canopy of green boughs erected on the school grounds. Here was tabled in luxurious profusion all that could tempt the appetite or please the palate of the most fastidious epicure. The good housekeepers of San Ramon will admit that justice was done their fare. After heartily refreshing the "inner man," all returned to the school room. This, during dinner, had been cleared for dancing.

At 1-30 P.M. the first dance was called. From that time till 4:30 P.M. those who were so inclined tripped it on the "light fantastic" to their hearts' content…The young people were not forgetful of their seniors. Occasionally the fancy dances gave place to a quadrille for the old folks.

It speaks well for the morality of San Ramon that no one appeared in Limerick on the 4th with the almost pardonable patriotic "brick in his hat." If any imbibed too freely that day they were discreet enough to remain invisible.

May the next Fourth be spent as pleasantly as this last.

HATTERAS

A *History of Contra Costa County* describes San Ramon in 1882 on page 444:

San Ramon

This is the name given to the Post-office at what is usually known as the village of Limerick, which we believe also once rejoiced in the name of Lynchville. It is situated in the lovely San Ramon valley, near its head, in the extreme south of the county, three miles above Danville, and eight from Hayward's in Alameda county.

For much of the nineteenth century, San Ramon was the largest community in the San Ramon Valley. When the Southern Pacific Railroad arrived in 1891, the large San Ramon station was placed one-half mile away from the village. This distance meant that the train's arrival didn't improve the village economy. The train station in Danville was near the center of town, which helped it became the valley's commercial center in the twentieth century.

A SCENE FROM SAN RAMON'S "HEY DAY" DATED 1850–1915

This drawing of old San Ramon is based on information researched and compiled by Sandee Wiedemann. The entire picture is displayed as a print on steel in the San Ramon main library.

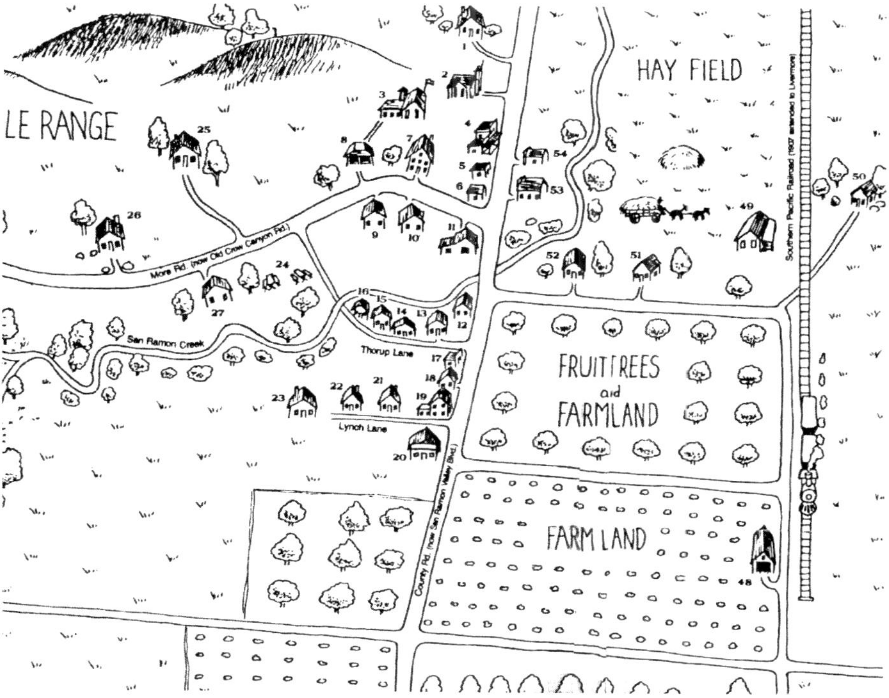

This drawing of San Ramon's "Hey Day" from 1850 to 1915 is based on several different sources. 1. McCamley home, 2. Methodist church, 3. School, 4. Hurst Store, 5. First Thorup shoe shop, 6. Chinese laundry, 7. Community hall (1911), 8. Shelter for horses, 9. Albertson home, 10. Olsson home, 11, Olsson blacksmith shop, 12. Barrett's saloon, 13. Frye home, 14. Redmond home, 15. Barrett home, 16. Griffin home, 17. Thorup shoe shop, 18. Thorup home, 19. San Ramon Hotel, 20. Tretzel saloon, 21. Lynch-Alexander home, 22. Lynch home, 24. Picnic grounds, 25. Swartz home, 26. Hanson home, 27. Erickson home, 49.Train depot, 53. Hogan home, 54. Mueller home. *Sandee Wiedemann collection.*

The Boulevard's Grande Dames Plus One

Every California community has its prominent homes, and nineteenth-century San Ramon was no exception. Five Grande Dames were distributed along the old highway that is now called San Ramon Valley Boulevard. The pioneer Wiedemann home, while not along the highway, is equally noteworthy.

The McCamley Home

San Ramon's most northerly home belonged to George and Ann McCamley (or McCamly). A large, two-story building, it was the first home in the village proper and was built by John White in 1852. After mining until 1855, McCamley bought the house and a ranch that extended east across San Ramon Creek. He was an important leader in San Ramon and the valley.

The *Illustrations of Contra Costa Co.* history book in 1879 described the property on page 21: "This ranch contains about 375 acres, valley and hill land, of good quality, and is devoted mostly to grain-raising, and produces large crops in good seasons. Magnificent mountain scenery surround the place in every direction; orchards, vineyards and scattered oaks form a picture of rare beauty from the residence."

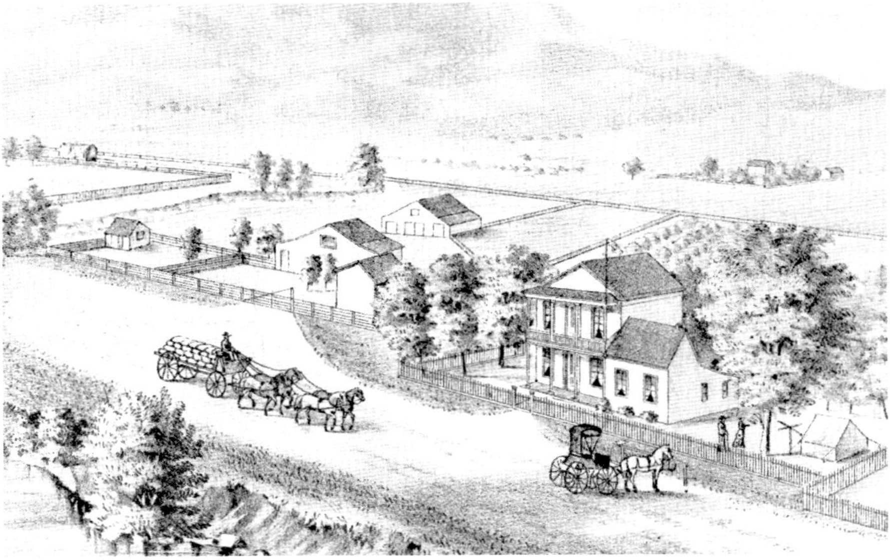

A drawing of the George and Ann McCamley home, taken from the *Illustrations of Contra Costa Co., California*, published in 1879. Built by John White in 1852, it was the first house in San Ramon village. *Museum of the San Ramon Valley.*

THE THORUP HOME

The Thorup home was located on five acres just south of the San Ramon Creek bridge next to the old highway. Peter and Anne Rasmussen Thorup were Danish immigrants (1868 and 1882) who married in 1884. Their two-story home had once been the C.C. Lewelling Hotel. In this home, the Thorups raised seven children. They helped many Danish relatives and friends move to America, hosting the new immigrants in their home for extended stays.

Thorup's custom boot and shoe shop was in San Ramon's village for fifty-five years and was patronized by everyone in the valley. Peter and Anne celebrated their fiftieth anniversary in 1934 and over two hundred people traveled to the Fraternal Hall in Danville to toast the couple and remember the Thorups' welcome to America.

The Thorup house lasted until the 1960s, when the old highway was reconfigured to accommodate the Crow Canyon Road off-ramp for Interstate 680.

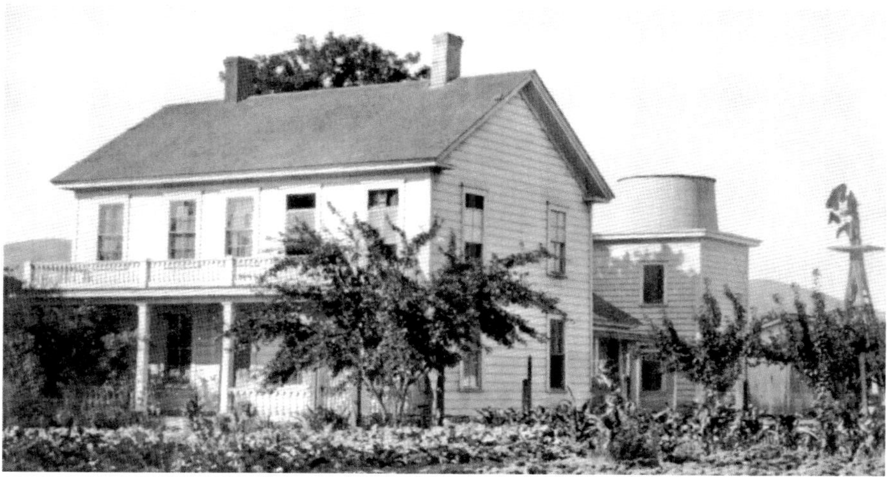

The two-story Anne and Peter Thorup home on San Ramon Valley Boulevard was once a hotel. This picture was taken around 1950. *Museum of the San Ramon Valley.*

THE HARLAN HOME, EL NIDO

This is the grandmother of historic houses along today's San Ramon Valley Boulevard and is one of the most storied of the Grande Dames, beginning with Joel Harlan's early involvement in the California Gold Rush. Minerva and Joel Harlan married in 1849 and moved to the San Ramon Valley in 1852. Minerva told her children there was so much gold around, she found it hard to believe that gold would be worth anything.

In 1857–58 they built a new Gothic Revival house, called "El Nido," which still sits at 19251 San Ramon Valley Boulevard in San Ramon. Furnishings were brought from the East Coast around Cape Horn. The Harlan house and gardens became landmarks, and the ranch was sometimes called Harlantan. The family was known for its geniality and hospitality. In 1870, their property was valued at $50,000.

An 1879 description of the Harlan place stated: "It is a two-story house, surrounded by ornamental and fruit trees. The yard has numerous walks, bordered by flowers and shrubs, and [is] kept in the most neat and tasteful manner."

Joel died in 1875, and Minerva ran the ranch for the next forty years. Their nine children were among the builders of young California. In

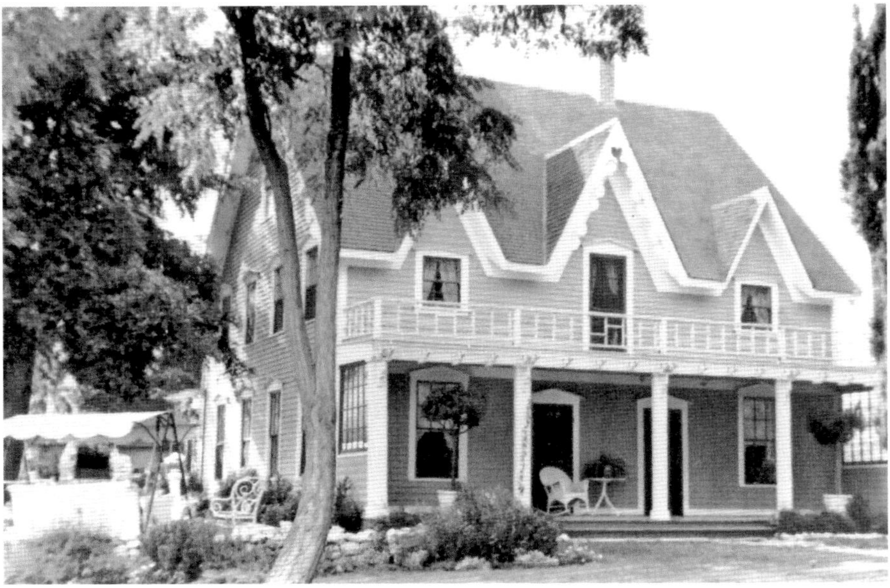

The Harlan home was built in 1858 and is the oldest building in San Ramon. Minerva and Joel Harlan built this Gothic Revival house. It was restored by their grandchildren in 1934. This picture was taken about 1940. *Museum of the San Ramon Valley.*

1934, some eighty years after its construction, the house and gardens were restored by Harlan descendants, the Geldermanns. It is the oldest house in San Ramon.

THE GLASS HOME

The Eliza and David Glass home was built next to the Harlan ranch. The Glasses came to Gold Rush California and established the first mercantile establishment south of Martinez, opening a store in Alamo during November 1850. In 1859, they moved south, purchased 718 acres from Leo Norris and started ranching.

In 1877, they built the elegant two-story Italianate that became their growing family's home. Their ranch headquarters eventually included the house, three barns, a worker's house, a granary, three hen houses, a windmill and a tank house. In 1870, the property was valued at $18,000. The 1879 *Illustrated Contra Costa County* history stated: "The residence is so situated,

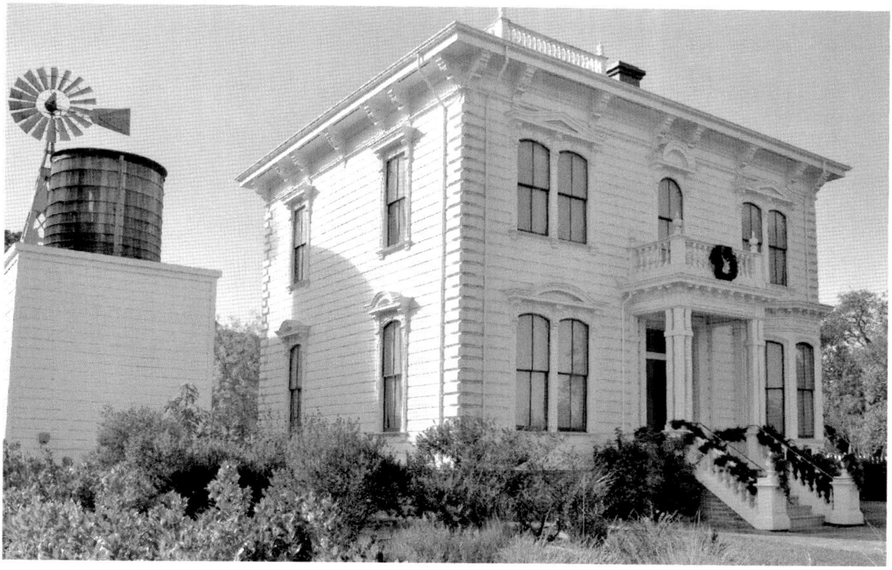

Eliza and David Glass built this Italianate home in 1877, nearly twenty years after they bought their San Ramon ranch. It was moved to Forest Home Farms Historic Park in 1998 and is now restored. This picture was taken in 2014. *Museum of the San Ramon Valley.*

from its commanding elevation, as to give a fine view of Mount Diablo, and of the surrounding country, for long distances."

The house was moved south to Forest Home Farms Historic Park in 1998. It has been beautifully restored and furnished by the city and is open to the public as a house museum.

THE BOONE HOME

The fifth Grande Dame was built in 1900 as a wedding present to themselves by Minnie and Numa Boone. A large two-story Dutch Colonial–style building with twenty-two rooms, the Boones surrounded it with a beautiful garden and nurtured ancient oaks, roses and olive trees on the property. The house and ranch buildings are located close to the county line. Samuel and Esther Russell were the first American owners of the property, and a Russell barn from the 1850s still survives.

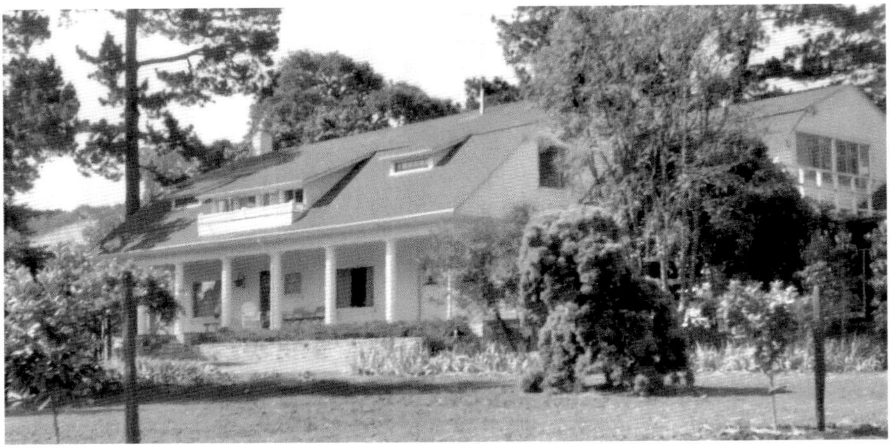

When Minnie Thorne and Numa Boone were married, she used an inheritance to build this two-story Dutch Colonial home in 1900. This picture was taken about 1920. *Museum of the San Ramon Valley.*

The Boones owned extensive ranch and orchard lands. Numa was president of the San Ramon Valley Bank and prominent in valley affairs. Today, their sixteen-acre headquarters buildings and land make up San Ramon's Forest Home Farms Historic Park, a gift to San Ramon in memory of Travis Boone by his wife, Ruth Quayle Boone, in 1997.

THE WIEDEMANN HOME

No description of San Ramon's Grande Dames is complete without noting the 1869 Wiedemann Home tucked into the western hills. This well-tended Gothic Revival house has been photographed and painted often and is a treasure with a long family history. The house is still lived in by a family descendant.

Christian Wiedemann and his partner moved to San Ramon in 1867 and began ranching on land west of the Norris League. He met Catherine Dittmer in Hayward, and they married in 1869. They had four children before she passed away in 1881. Wiedemanns have been active as ranchers and leaders in the area for well over one hundred years and at one point were the largest landowners in San Ramon.

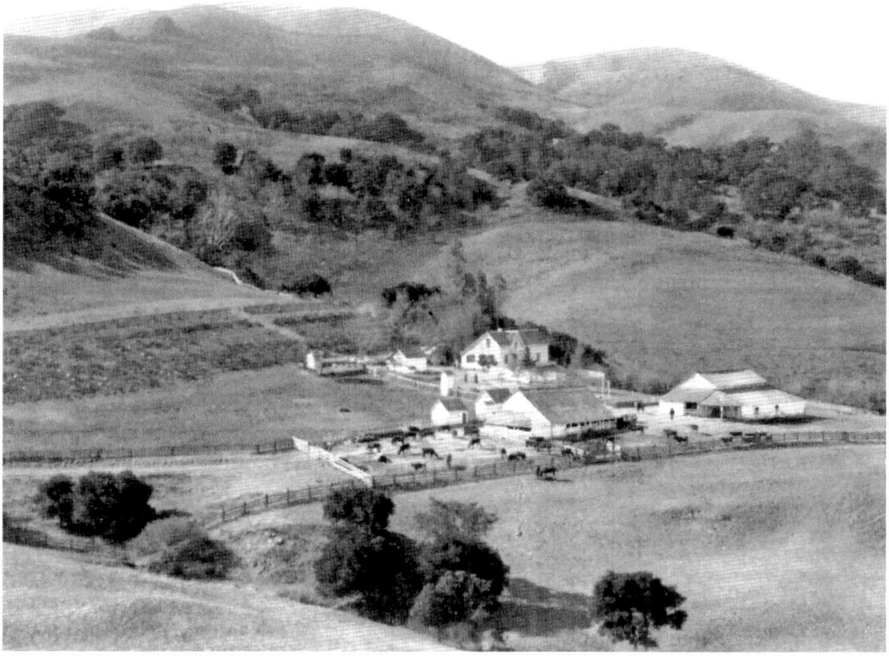

The Wiedemann house and barns are shown on San Ramon's western hills during the nineteenth century. *Museum of the San Ramon Valley.*

In 1926, a Contra Costa County history book described San Ramon and pointed out, "Some splendid places are to be found in this vicinity." All the "splendid places" owned by the McCamley, Thorup, Harlan, Glass, Boone and Wiedemann families were regularly noted by travelers and appeared on early maps of San Ramon. In the twenty-first century, the two northern Grande Dames are no more, but fortunately, the Harlan, Wiedemann, Glass and Boone homes remain as vivid reminders of the community's proud past.

And Here's San Ramon—in 1880

Letter from San Ramon in the *Contra Costa Gazette*, March 9, 1880:

Eds. Gazette:

Thinking that a few items from our locality might be of interest, we will commence by saying that the crop prospects are upon the whole on average with former years at this season. The earlier sown grain has suffered some from the ravages of worms, but the more experienced farmers seem to think that we are over the worst on that score, as we are having some warm days at present. We had yesterday and during the night, up to the present writing, 2. P.M., a genuine norther, which makes an occasional hole in some old dilapidated fence, also did some damage to Mr. Geo. McPheters' windmill—of which we will speak further on. All the weather prophets predict that another pluvial outpouring will follow in the wake of "old boreas," judging from one similar which occurred about eight years since, and if we should have the expected storm to add to our already eleven inches of rain, we would certainly expect an abundant harvest.

We will now leave our grain fields and see what is doing in our village of San Ramon, in which there are indications of a revival in business. Of something new, we will give a passing notice to all. Mr. Jas. Barrett, proprietor of the San Ramon Valley Hotel, keeps an average country establishment, and as there is no drinking saloon kept in the house, we think that the proprietor deserves some commendation. Next comes Mr. Pat Horan's place of business, where any one inclined may libate to his satisfaction, as he constantly keeps on hand an average article of genuine tangleleg, and judging from the number of drunks we would say that he seems to be doing a big business. Next in order is B.W. Dorn & Co., who keeps a well supplied country store, and who tells us that they are doing a very fair business, but expect a still better in the near future. Mr. P.A. Thorpe, across the way, keeps a neat boot and shoe shop; has a business that keeps two men constantly at work.

We will pass by our Chinese wash house, that none seem to care for save for the clean linen they turn out. Following in succession is L.B. Brigham, who has quite a large and commodious building, erected for a paint shop, but only for a short time did he wield the brush till he laid it aside for the fascinating glass, and lo and behold! The new paint shop is convaried into what must be called a first class village saloon, where our boys have all the inducements that such places offer, held out to them to congregate and take their first lessons in the downward road to ruin, and then there seems to be a great number who are availing themselves of thus taking their first steps to ruin and degradation. Of course there is no use remonstrating with the proprietors of these places, as they will point behind their well arranged bars at their lawful license, claiming that they are engaged in a legitimate business.

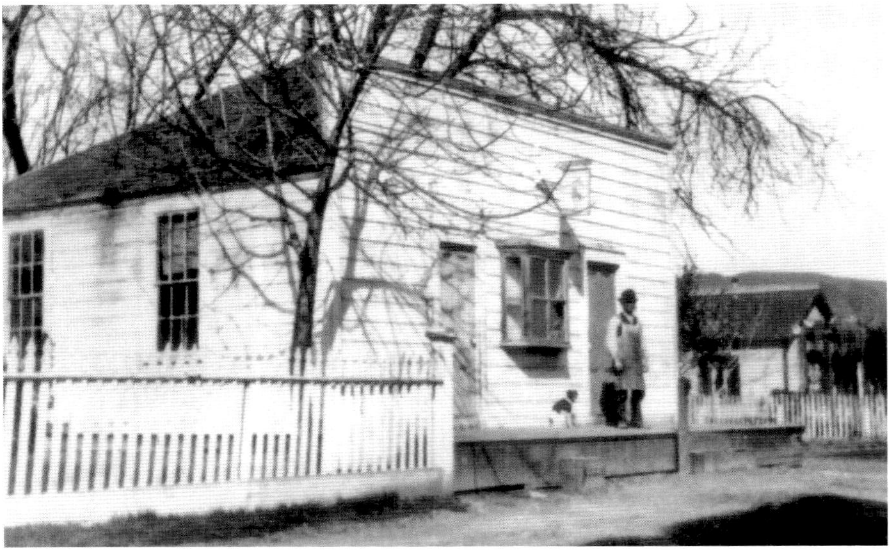

Peter Thorup appears on the porch outside his shoe and boot store on the old highway just north of the San Ramon Creek bridge. He opened the shop in 1875 and ran it for fifty-five years. *Museum of the San Ramon Valley.*

We will now cross the San Ramon Bridge to one of the oldest blacksmith shops in the country, first established in 1860 by E. Brewen, and conducted by his two older sons since his decease, some five years ago, they being mere boys at the time of their father's death, but by their perseverance they have supported a large family and have a good business, well established.

Patience, Mr. Editor, our next is another drinking saloon, presided over by a Mr. Jas. Norris, and the description and business is very much like the two former spoken of. Our next is a new store under the firm name of Glass & Ivory (good material in the name). Mr. Frank Glass, a son of Mr. David Glass, and Mr. E. Ivory, who is well known throughout the country, are the partners. Mrs. Ivory, with the junior partner, are presiding over the business in the absence of her husband, who is expected from Washington Territory, where they emigrated some two years ago.

Next Mr. Geo. McPheters' blacksmith, wheelwright and paint shop. Mr. McPheters has shown considerable ingenuity in the construction of a huge windmill, which measures sixty feet in circumference, and of which we have made mention as being slightly damaged during the late windstorm; one of the fans was torn off. We have also just learned that Mr. J. Smith's barn was unroofed.

The next is our school house, of which we feel some pride, as it will accommodate one hundred scholars comfortably, and presided over by Mr. E.J. Root and Miss Maggie McMahon. School opened last Monday morning.

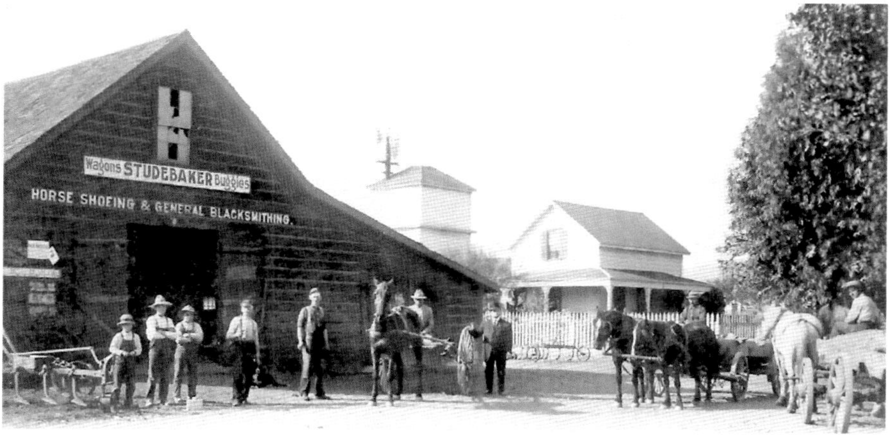

Andrew Olsson's blacksmith shop was located in San Ramon village along the old highway. *Pictured left to right*: Edwin Olsson, Reuben Olsson, unknown, Andrew Olsson, Oscar Olsson, Fred Wiedemann, Mark McIvor and two other unknown men. *Museum of the San Ramon Valley.*

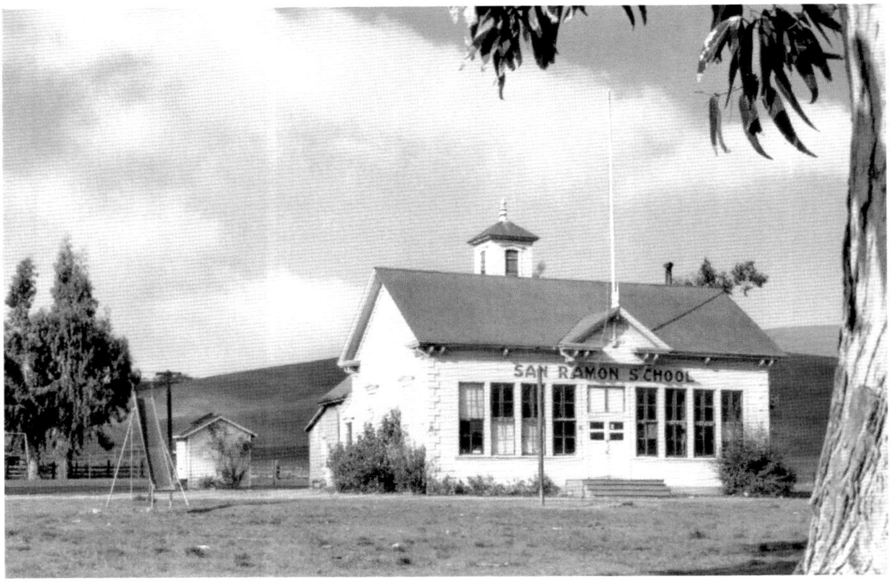

The San Ramon Grammar School was built in 1867 and served the community until a new elementary school was constructed in 1950. *Museum of the San Ramon Valley.*

Now last but not least as an item, Mr. G.K. Taylor has been lecturing for the past month, and delivered in all eight lectures, outlining one hundred and eight under the Blue Ribbon pledge, and has organized an Encampment of Temperance Cavaliers, this being the first Lodge of the Order ever organized. Following are the names of the charter members of Alpha Encampment No. 1:

D.A. Caldwell, Geo. McPheters, A.L. Stephens, M.L. Simpson, F.B. More, G.B. Dales, Chas. Noyes, Mrs. C. Ivory, Mrs. A. Stephens, H. Russell, W.A. Greer, Miss Jennie Grist, Miss Dora Dobson, Miss Jennie Horan, Geo. Wood, Juo. Camp, Mrs. F. Wood.

The following is the list of officers: D.A. Caldwell, C. of L.; Chas. Noyes, F.L.; M.L. Simpson, T.L.; Geo. McPheters, M. of C.; F.B. More, K. of E.; G.B. Dales, L. of G.; Miss Jennie Horan, W.; A.L. Stephens, D.; W.A. Greer, V.; Miss Jennie Grist, C. of R.

Cavalier
(Editor's note: clearly, a temperance man)

Bishop Ranch in the Heart of San Ramon

The Bishop name has been a significant one in San Ramon since Thomas Benton Bishop acquired the property in 1895 from the Norris family. Leo and Mary Jane Norris had purchased their 4,550-acre ranch from Jose Maria Amador forty-five years earlier.

Thomas Bishop bought the property after a scandalous divorce case between William and Margaret Norris in which Margaret was represented by an attorney from the San Francisco firm of Garber, Boalt and Bishop. Evidently, Norris land was accepted in payment for services rendered, and Bishop, a partner in the firm, purchased the land from her attorney.

Bishop already owned land throughout the west and Mexico. The Norris settlement property was one and a half square miles (960 acres) and extended from Norris Canyon on the west to the Southern Pacific Railroad track on the east.

In 1904, Bishop hired the experienced Frank Rutherford to manage the ranch. Rutherford and James H. Bishop, who became president of the company after his father died in 1906, worked together for forty years. Bishop's four sons, James, Francis, Edward and Thomas, inherited the estate. The ranch was sometimes called the Bishop Brothers Ranch or the San Ramon Rancho.

Rutherford brought expertise in the grafting and propagation of different varieties of fruit and nut trees. Orchards of native black walnut trees were planted on the Bishop Ranch beginning in 1909. These young trees were grafted with English varieties three or four years later. As these

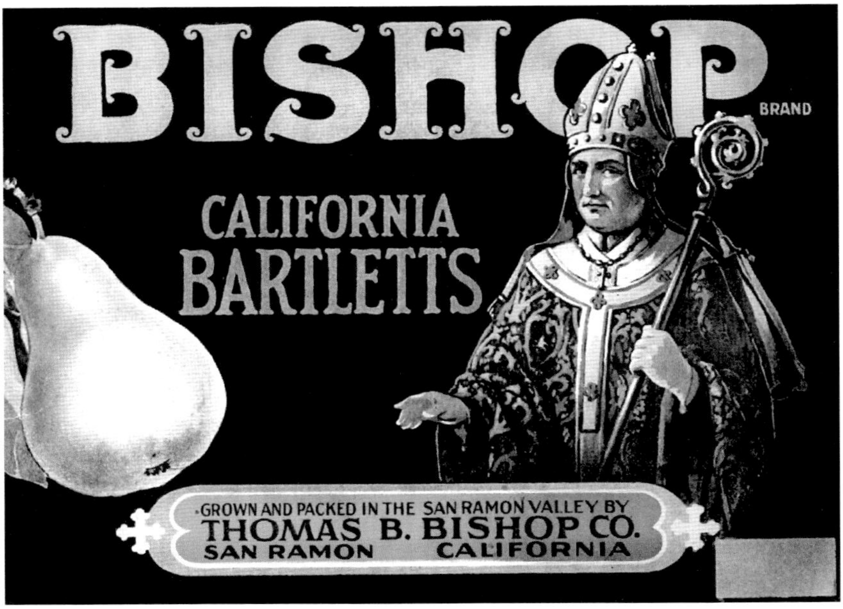

This Bishop Ranch lithograph shows a bishop on the label. It would have been glued to a wooden fruit box to identify the premier Bartlett pears that were shipped from Bishop Ranch. *Museum of the San Ramon Valley.*

early plantings succeeded on five hundred acres, many more orchards were planted in the San Ramon and adjacent valleys.

Gradually, the ranch became a huge, successful enterprise, in part because it had the only irrigation in the valley. It had a bunkhouse for about sixty men, barns, machine shops, dehydrator buildings, warehouses and a mess hall. Bartlett pears were planted in 1911, as were peaches, prunes, grapes and tomatoes. From 1900 to 1920, the ranch was well known for its prize-winning pure-bred Shropshire sheep, a project of Edward F. Bishop. At the 1915 Panama-Pacific International Exposition, the sheep took double "the number of firsts and as many seconds as all the other exhibitors combined. They also took the honor of Champion Ram, Premier Champion for Exhibitor, and Premier Championship for Breeder."

Here Bishop Brothers Ranch is touted in the *Gazette Contra Costa Development* newspaper of 1916:

> *San Ramon Ranch is at once a demonstration of the perfection of natural conditions which exist not only conducive to the live stock industry, but*

appertaining to horticulture and farming pursuits in general. It is a portrayal of the scenic beauties of this section of the State that is at once a surprise and a delight, for its vast expanse entails the rolling landscape of the foothills and the wealth of Contra Costa valley lands. They are both combined here in perfection.

Evidently, coyotes would come down from the hills and kill the Bishop Ranch lambs and sheep. Rutherford kept six greyhounds to prevent such depredation. If a coyote was spotted, the driver of one of their large steam tractors would blow a whistle. A worker closest to the kennel would release the hounds, which would come tearing out in the direction of the whistle, run down the coyotes and kill them.

It was a diversified and self-sufficient ranch with various fruit crops, walnuts, blooded sheep, hogs, chickens, a large vegetable garden, numerous

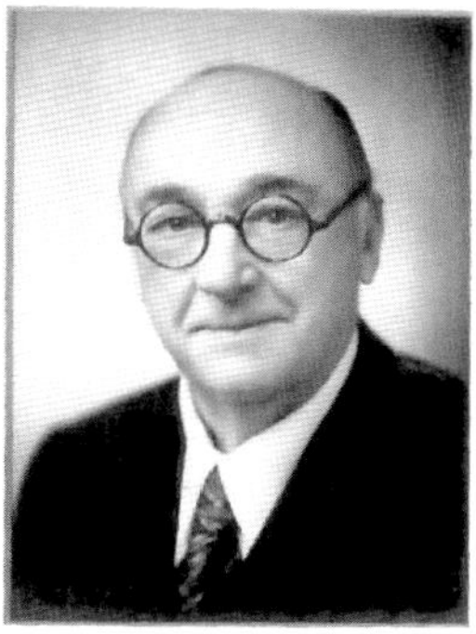
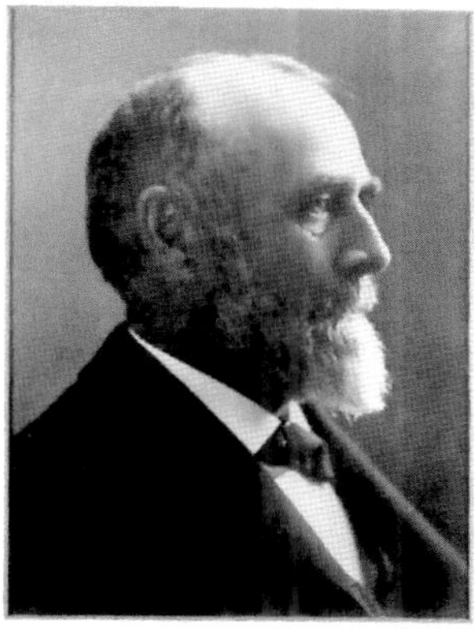
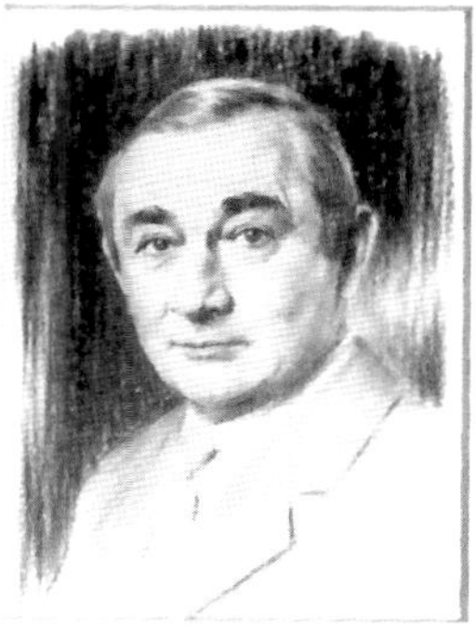
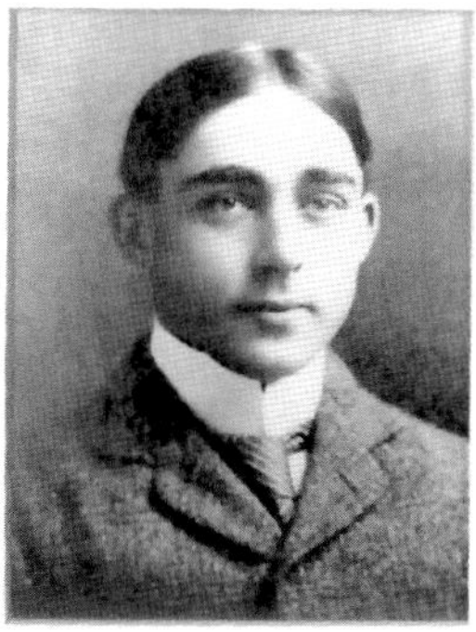
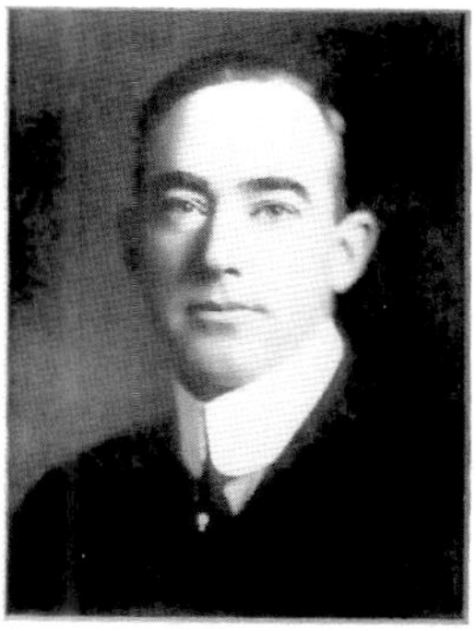

Thomas B. Bishop is surrounded by his four sons, who inherited his many properties. James H. Bishop (upper left) was president of the Bishop Brothers Ranch for forty years. *Museum of the San Ramon Valley.*

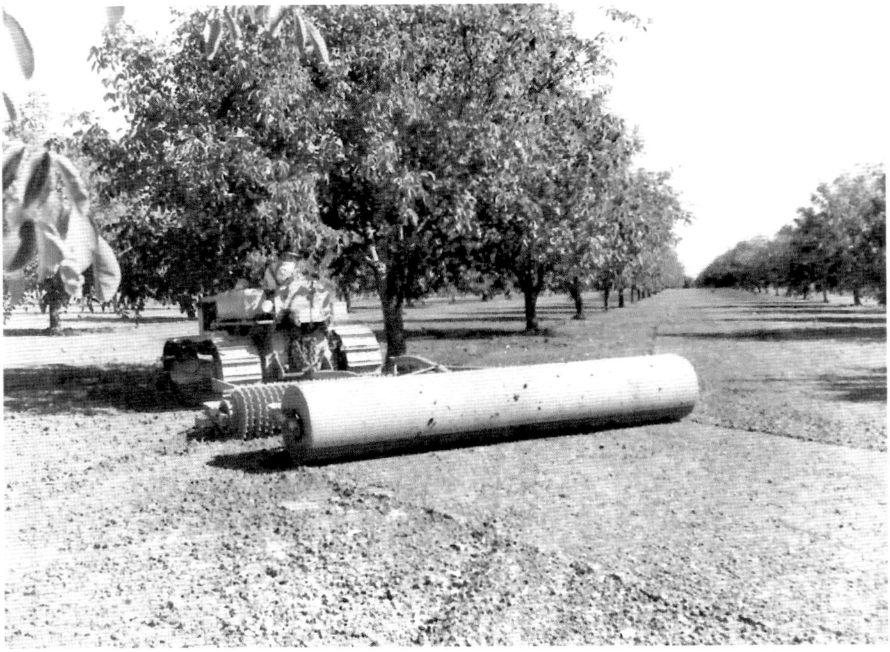

A Caterpillar D4 tractor is pulling a combination drag, ring-roller and smooth roller to prepare the walnut orchard floor for harvest at Bishop Ranch. *Museum of the San Ramon Valley.*

workers and a variety of ranch buildings. Early experimental mechanical walnut harvesters were also tested in the Bishop orchard.

According to Barbara Andreasen Lynch, "There were two migrant worker 'labor camps' on the ranch; one was known as the Chinese camp. Each had a communal kitchen and the seasonal canning was done at the labor camp rather than the main crew kitchen."

In the late 1940s, the Bishop Ranch (described as 1,300 acres in size) was recognized in the *Guinness Book of World Records* as having the largest single Bartlett pear orchard in the world; it yielded 2,200 tons one year out of 300 acres. By then, the ranch had three irrigation wells that supported the pears and walnuts. Pears were sent to East Coast markets and to the Del Monte Cannery in Hayward, with small ones sent to the Davis cannery in Walnut Creek to be made into baby food.

Travis and Ruth Boone owned a large spread adjacent to Bishop Ranch, planted primarily with walnuts and tomatoes. Boone did extensive custom grain harvesting in the San Ramon and Tri-Valley area. In a later interview,

Ruth Boone recalled that, after bachelor ranch hands were paid, they would often enjoy themselves gambling at a place called Connie's in San Ramon. She remembered Connie Young telling her, "I made a fortune from the men at the Boone and Bishop Ranches." And she said he probably was right.

Following Rutherford's retirement in 1944, his son-in-law Vern Andreasen became manager, and in 1955, Bob Livermore succeeded him. He was a University of California–Davis graduate with some new ideas for the ranch. Livermore faced a number of challenges. Crop dusting had ended, and pests were re-infesting many of the crops. Pear decline and black-line diseases threatened the ranch's pears and walnuts. In the 1950s, Henry Crown and Co. purchased the property.

The Bay Area's growth after World War II transformed all of California. In the San Ramon Valley, owners of several historic ranches were confronted with high tax assessments that meant they could not afford to continue ranching. The Baldwin and Meese Ranches, which were first settled in 1852, were sold to home developers. Bishop Ranch taxes in 1955 were about $20,000, but ten years later, the assessor valued the land for homes and the tax bill skyrocketed.

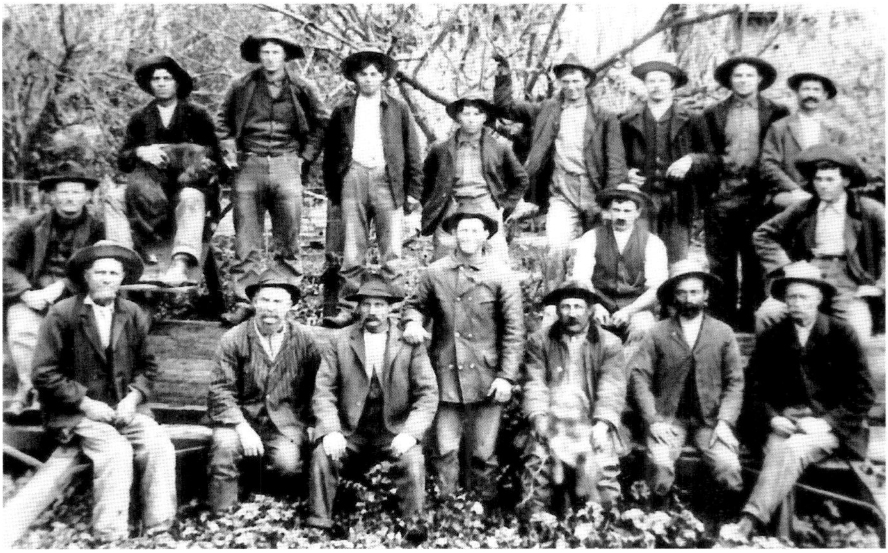

The Bishop Ranch was a large, diversified ranch. Workers lived in bunkhouses and ate at the mess hall. They planted a variety of fruits and tomatoes, tended walnut and pear orchards and raised cattle, sheep and hogs (photo circa 1920). *Museum of the San Ramon Valley.*

Aerial pictures showed the central position of Bishop Ranch in the '60s. Its sweeping pear and walnut orchards sat between new developments in South San Ramon and Dublin and a growing Danville to the north. The entire San Ramon Valley expanded from 4,630 people in 1950 to 57,307 in 1980.

New residents soon began to want more control of these burgeoning developments, and incorporation efforts began in the 1960s with three unsuccessful San Ramon Valley–wide city votes. Whether to include the Bishop Ranch property within the proposed city boundary was debated in each of these elections.

The life of Bishop Ranch as the agricultural center of San Ramon ended when Western Electric purchased the 1,733-acre property from Crown Enterprises in 1969 and proceeded to plan for a "new town" development.

Henry Wiedemann's San Ramon Memories

In 1956, Roxanne Wiedemann asked her great-uncle Henry to write about San Ramon history. Here are some excerpts from his letters:

Early days in San Ramon and vicinity, as I viewed them as a boy. It is interesting to some people to know something of the facts concerning the community in which they live. I was born Apr. 10, 1872 about three miles south west of San Ramon near the county line of Contra Costa and Alameda on the ranch which my father acquired in 1865.

Ranching

Previous to the coming of the '49ers, the country was still open range and unfenced and cattle would run at large. Cattle raising was the principle occupation those days and everyone's cattle would run together, so the owners would have a roundup or rodeo to use the Spanish term. The different owners would gather their cattle together, and cut out whichever animals had their brand and earmark, and any increase in the herd would also be branded and earmarked. When the rodeo was over they would pick out a maverick—that is an animal that no one claimed—and have a barbecue feast. This was the rodeo from the business point of view.

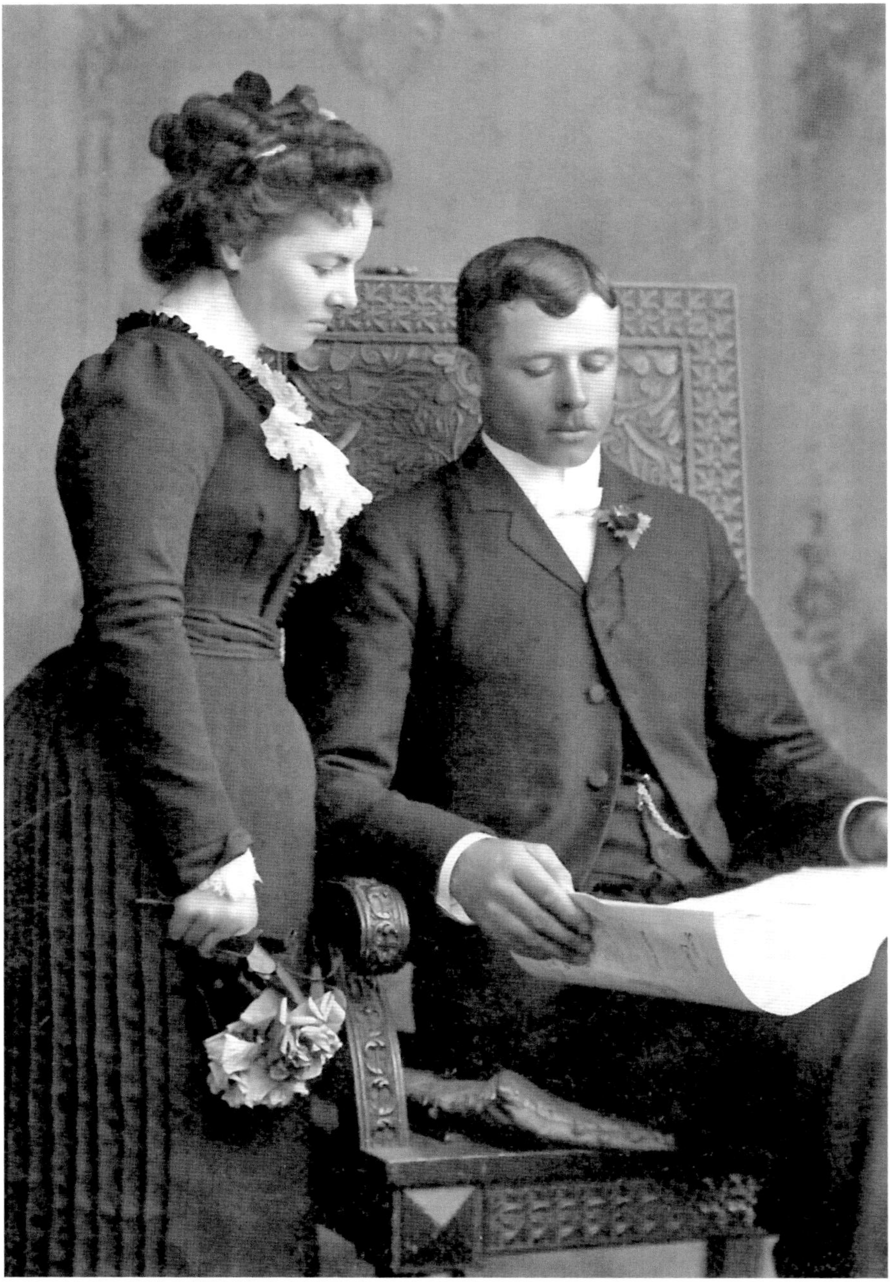

A young Henry and Elvina Wiedemann are shown in this picture. Henry lived in San Ramon most of his life. *Wiedemann family collection.*

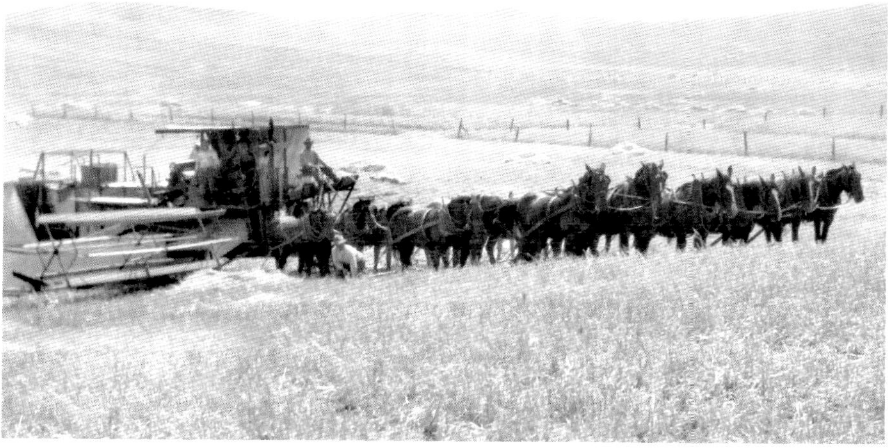

Wiedemann's gasoline-powered combined harvester apparently stopped for a hitch repair and photo. Sixteen to twenty-four horses (depending on how steep the hills were) pulled the machine through the grain fields before dependable crawler tractors became available, circa 1925. *Wiedemann family collection.*

In later years when the ranches were fenced, there wasn't much occasion any more with few exceptions, so it [the rodeo] almost ceased to be practical any more. So to perpetuate its glamour and the colorful western features associated with it, it became one of the nation's greatest sports.

A CREEK DIVERTED

The creek known as the San Ramon Creek that flows through the town of San Ramon has its main source in Bollinger Canyon. It also carries the water from Norris Canyon which it originally did not. The water from the Norris Canyon was diverted from a point a short distance below the George Norris residence and went straight to the San Ramon Creek a short distance above the old Lynch home. Originally the water from the Norris Canyon flowed in the general direction of the Bishop Ranch and spread over quite a large area during a flood and especially over the Lynch field on the east side of the highway.

San Ramon in the 1880s

San Ramon as I first remember it as a youngster going to school, was similar to most of the country towns of that time. Not being a mining town, the chief occupation was farming and cattle raising. At the time that I refer to, it had two blacksmith shops, a shoe maker shop, two stores, three hotels, four bars, a Chinese laundry and school house and livery stable. San Ramon in those earlier days had some of the glamour of a typical frontier town as far as law and order was concerned. Quite a contrast as of today.

Sometimes a customer in a hilarious frame of mind would disregard all saloon etiquette and take a short cut to the bar on horseback for the amusement of the crowd.

Blacksmiths who did business here at different times were Brewen, Jay Dutchee, George McPheters, Jake Buttner. They were among the earliest. Later there was Erickson and Albertsen, Webster, Fry, and Olsson. San Ramon also had a resident doctor for a number of years, Dr. G.E. Alexander, a G.A.R. veteran and son-in-law of William Lynch, an early pioneer settler. There were two other doctors of an earlier period, Dr. Labaree and Dr. Dragou.

A Memorable Party

One event in San Ramon that was always outstanding to the old time Democrats was when Grover Cleveland was elected president for his first term [1885]. Being the first Democratic president to be elected in twenty years the Demos were so elated over the outcome of the election and to give vent to their hilarity they must celebrate by throwing a barbeque. One of the local Demos felt so jubilant that he contributed a whole beef for the occasion.

This took place in the San Ramon School yard. A speakers platform was erected in front of the schoolhouse. The event began by firing off anvils…The principle speaker of the day was John P. Irish, a notable political figure of that era. After that spell binding speech, the main objective then was to join the hungry throng to the big feed that awaited them, and what a feed, served in regular barbeque style which they attacked with a vengeance…they rounded out [the day] with a grand parade through town led by John Camp and a prominent lady of San Ramon.

By 1865 there were roads between San Ramon and Hayward for horse drawn vehicles. They were very narrow through the deep canyons, very muddy in the winter time and dusty in the summer. Before that traveling was mostly by horseback and pack horses were used to quite an extent. Some of the old trails are still visible.

Chinese in San Ramon

Then there was the Chinese laundry, nearly every town had them, San Ramon was no exception, it had two at one time, not too sanitary. It was the custom those days for Chinese to wear cues or pig tails as they were generally called which hung down their back in a long braid. They could smoke opium unmolested. Many of the ranchers employed them as cooks and also in the harvest time to bind grain as the self-binding machines were not yet in general use.

Although they were very peaceable, they were always a target for the boys, playing pranks which often got them into trouble some times but the sight of that gun that some of the Chinese had up their sleeve caused them to change their minds.

There was a certain element throughout California arousing the people to the detriment of the cheap coolie labor. They, also, had an Anti-Chinese league in San Ramon which led to many heated arguments as they were about equally divided for and against the League. But it was not long before the excitement subsided and things got back to normal again.

San Ramon Grammar School

The old San Ramon School, which still stands, having out-lived its usefulness as a school house is one of San Ramon's most outstanding land marks to bring back fond memories of by-gone days. It served many other purposes besides dispensing the three R's, as a meeting place for all occasions until the San Ramon Hall was built later, San Ramon was noted for its high class of entertainment by the pupils and local talent, and was looked forward to as a great event, which in fact it was.

The school could also be converted into a sizable ballroom by taking out the partitions and its fame as a dance hall, also the scene of maskerades, was country-wide. This was about 1880. Some of the scholars rode horseback and [others] walked two to four miles to school.

A San Ramon boy to win fame as a brilliant scholar graduated from San Ramon School in 1889 to become a noted educator and attorney and figured preeminently in many law departments, was once a candidate for Governor of California. Judge William H. Langdon became one of the most outstanding jurists in California…He, also, had some serious decisions to make that I heard him remark in a speech he delivered in San Ramon Hall. His problem was that his mother would have to sacrifice for him to acquire a high education or choose to follow the plow. His brilliant record is a good proof of which way he decided to go.

Quite a number of the scholars in the old days rode horseback to school, about twenty or more. Many being raised in that environment of horse back riding made racing a general thing among old and young alike. It seemed to be in the blood. There was always a keen rivalry as to who had the fastest horse [and] of course that had to be settled by running a race, usually through the town, amid the plaudits of the spectators. There were two training tracks in the valley used principally for harness racing.

MAKING A LIVING

Bollinger Canyon which still retains the name, was settled in the early fifties by Joshua Bollinger, a native of Missouri. He acquired a large tract of land on the Canyon, as they were a pioneering class of people. Finally more and more of his people settled in the Canyon. They were a generous and hospitable class of people. Their favorite pastime was whittling at which they were very adept. Owing to their pioneering habits, they did not acquire much schooling, which sometimes put them in some amusing situations.

At the early period, farming was carried on quite extensively so there was always a lot of activity in and out of town. When farming equipment was all horse drawn, that required a large number of ranch hands.

There was a constable, Bert Reed, who had a jail across the road from the tire house. Bert received $1.50 for every prisoner, so consequently every vagrant spent at least one night in the jail's one room.

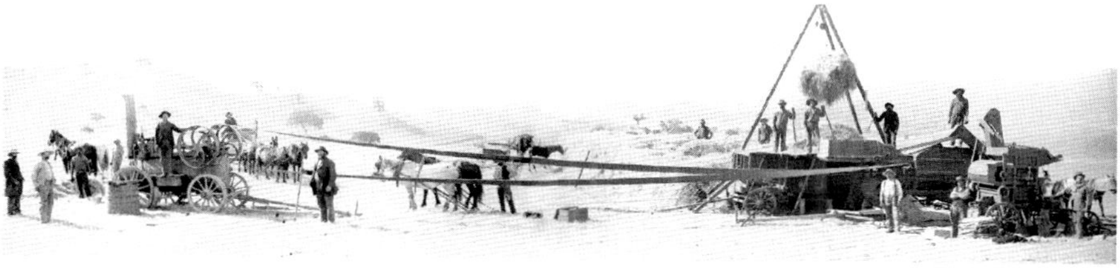

In this picture, a straw-fired steam engine is powering a stationary threshing machine with a grain cleaner alongside. Horses are used to bring water for the engine and other functions. Joshua Bollinger is shown in the middle of this picture in a suit and hat with a walking stick. *Museum of the San Ramon Valley.*

With poor transportation, very few would go away from town so there always was a lot of activity especially on Sundays when big crowds would gather. Among a large crowd there are always some unique characters like the miner with the long flowing beard who didn't strike pay dirt, yearning for the millions in "them thar hills" and the man with the glazed eyes with the periodical illusions that he laid the foundation of "Frisco."

It would be a dull day if there were not a few brawls occasionally. San Ramon still retains some of that western atmosphere.

The 1906 Earthquake and Fire Light Up the Western Sky

The most significant Bay Area event of the early twentieth century was the April 18, 1906 San Francisco earthquake and fire. This disaster dispersed people into other Bay Area locations and left indelible memories on San Ramon residents

The *Report of the State Earthquake Commission* in 1908 stated that in San Ramon "most chimneys fell. San Ramon Saloon, south of the bridge, slid off its foundations, window panes were broken. Neither church nor school-house suffered any damage. The shock was mostly in a north–south direction." Evidently Peter Thorup's chimney was one that fell off.

Elsie Fereira Valentine recalled what happened to her family. The Fereiras lived in Bollinger Canyon and, since so many chimneys had fallen or cracked after the quake, her father, Manuel, had their chimney inspected by an expert, who pronounced it sound. When they lit the first fire that fall, the entire house burned down.

Eight-year-old Astrid Olsson, whose family had a blacksmith shop and house in the village, said that the quake and aftershocks were terrifying. The family pulled bedding outside and slept on the porch during the many temblors for fear the house would collapse. She remembered that the entire sky to the west was illuminated by the San Francisco fire.

Another family's story recounts Fred Wiedemann riding to the top of Wiedemann Hill to watch the fire from there. One member said he brought a chair along.

As it happened, Ramona Park, a new public picnic grounds, was scheduled to open April 26, 1906, on the Meese Ranch property next to

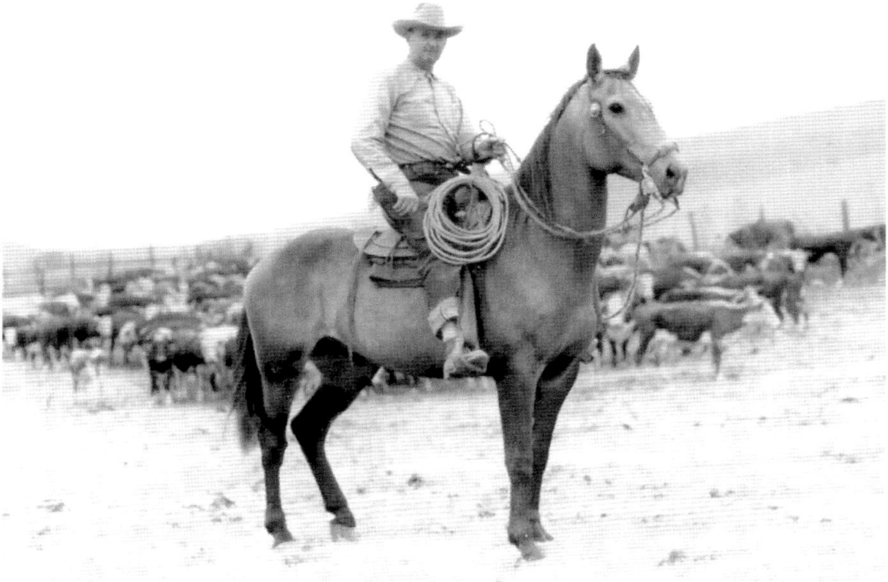

Fred Wiedemann is shown on his horse Gil Blas in 1937. He would have been twenty-seven when he rode up Wiedemann hill during the San Francisco fire. *Wiedemann family collection.*

the Southern Pacific Railroad line. The park was just north of San Ramon Village and inside the San Ramon Grammar School district, where the Greenbrook condominiums stand today. The quake and fire cancelled the grand opening as people mobilized to assist the thousands of refugees flowing out of the city. The park opening was postponed to July 4.

Ramona Park was designed to be used by large groups, which could take the railroad to the valley. The *Martinez Daily Gazette* recorded: "Residents of this county are looking forward to Thursday, April 26, when Ramona Park, located at the foot of Mt. Diablo in the beautiful San Ramon Valley and said to be one of the prettiest parks in this State, will open."

A *Gazette* article on April 18 assured readers that "it will undoubtedly be recognized in a short while, as the first of California's many parks for pleasure seekers, excepting possibly the Golden Gate Park, though there the hand of man, a poor imitator, is more manifest than that of nature." Picnickers were invited to the ten-acre park, which was "covered with wild maple, buckeye, elder and other California trees, and with a picturesque little lake…ideal for

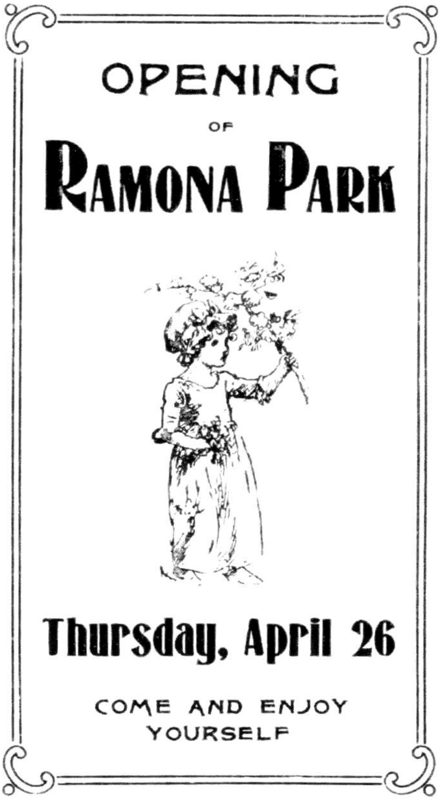

Left: This brochure showing a sweet girl was produced for the group park's original opening in April 1906. *Museum of the San Ramon Valley.*

Below: The Ramona Park sign greeted visitors to the area, circa 1920. *Contra Costa County Historical Society.*

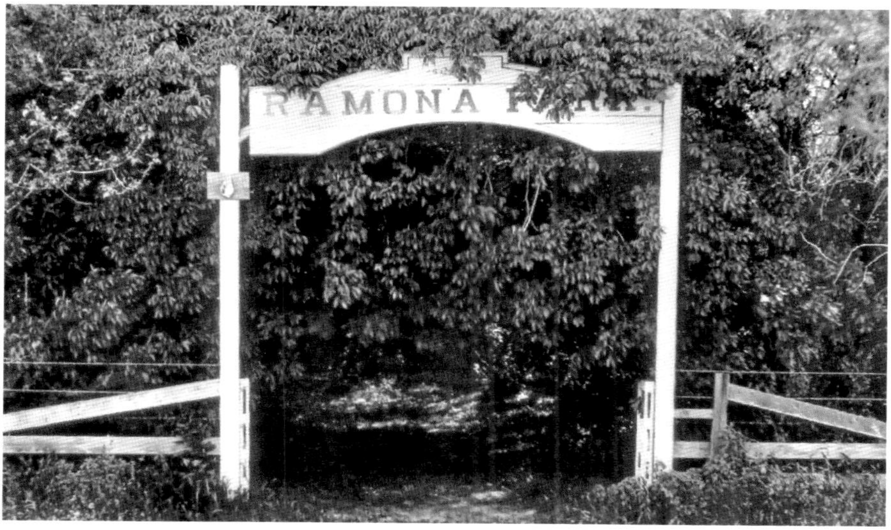

swimming." There was a fine dancing pavilion "whose floor no means have been spared to make perfect."

Because "temperance principles" (no liquor) were to be followed in and around the park, women and children were assured "perfect freedom from the insults of drunken bums."

The June 29, 1906 *Daily Gazette* reported, "Hundreds of places have quite a reputation for beauty that have not a tenth of the beauty of this place, and all lovers of exquisite scenery will be gratified by going there."

When the park did open on July 4, 25 percent of the receipts for the day were sent to the earthquake relief committee, a decision taken by the Ramona Park committee, which included B.W. Stone, B.W. Bennett, A.J. Abbott, J.S. Patton and Ralph Dobson. Admission to the grounds was free, and a special train left San Francisco at 8:00 a.m., stopping at all intervening stations, and leaving the park at 5:00 p.m.

The day's program was planned by the Danville Lodge No. 378, Independent Order of Odd Fellows, with a special dispensation granted by the lodge's grand master to allow all members to wear their regalia in public.

Ramona Park was a popular place for local outings for decades. Rose Ferreira of Tassajara remembers going there in a horse and buggy for picnics with her family as a young girl. The new high school had regular year-end parties at the park. Bill Fereira, who lived in San Ramon Village, recalled Japanese soldiers coming for a picnic in the 1930s.

Happily, this unique group park is not forgotten. A modern Ramona Park is now located in San Ramon's Dougherty Valley.

The Twentieth Century Marches On

San Ramon went through the highs and lows of twentieth-century living as horses were replaced with tractors and cars, young men were lost in two world wars, electricity transformed everything and the radio brought up-to-date news to people's living rooms.

In 1911, California women won the vote after a vigorous campaign. Female leaders in San Ramon were already energetic and well respected. Anita and Loretta Glass ran the Lora Nita (Glass) Ranch, and Minnie Lynch and Mary Wiedemann helped create the new San Ramon Hall. Several civic-spirited women served on the San Ramon Committee for the memorable 1915 Panama-Pacific International Exposition that opened in San Francisco: Mary Llewellyn, Ramona Read, Anita Thorup, Elmina Harlan, Nellie Hurst, Anita Glass and Susan Rutherford. Local men on the committee were Frank Rutherford, Numa Boone, H.C. Hurst, William Meese, Oscar Olsson and George Oswill.

On June 5, 1917, saloons were closed, and men registered for military service in the Great War. San Ramon had 21 men register, Alamo 22, Tassajara 28 and Danville 107. Local volunteers sold bonds to support the war effort, including Fred Wiedemann, William Meese and Harry Hurst. Boys went off to the world wars in Europe and returned with new perspectives. San Ramon's Lloyd Wood and Simeon Anderson died in the war.

At the small downtown, the grammar school and San Ramon Hall provided centers for the community. William C. Fereira purchased the San

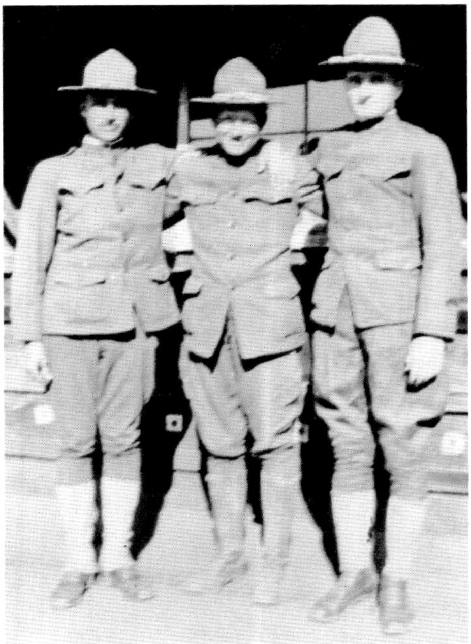

Three San Ramon doughboys at Camp Kearney, San Diego, February 17, 1918. *Left to right*: Romie Thorup, Lloyd Wood and Noel Norris. *Museum of the San Ramon Valley.*

Ramon General Store in 1924 (for $2,750) and added gas station service. At the store, there were unending card games played until the wee hours of the morning. Bill Fereira recalled his father's place as a refuge for bachelor ranch workers. "They'd all converge at the store every night. They'd play cribbage or poker."

Prohibition in the '20s meant that the local saloons closed down. But several enterprising Italians produced alcohol in barns along Crow and Cull Canyons, often under the guise of being chicken ranchers. Evidently, Bellina Canyon, just a mile over the county line into Alameda County off Crow Canyon Road, had a cluster of these stills. Bruno Buti wrote a book about his father's success at making a high-quality whiskey called Jackass brandy that some locals appreciated since they preferred whiskey to water.

During the Depression, ranchers had more land than cash. Travis Boone and his new wife, Ruth, moved to the home ranch in 1930 and worked to revitalize the Boone family's Forest Home Farms as his father, Numa, declined in health. Ruth said they sold jars of special orange and grapefruit marmalade, pickles and salted almonds with the label "Forest Home Food Specials" during weekends. These sales provided the only cash they saw for years.

Pearl Harbor shook everybody. Ann Wiedemann Kaplan recalled the attack vividly. She and her family listened to reports on the radio all that day. Her brother Howard was too tall to serve in the navy. She and a girlfriend watched for Japanese airplanes in the small San Ramon Air Watch building next to the Fereiras' general store. All the local Japanese Americans were taken away that spring: "One day they were here, the next day they were gone."

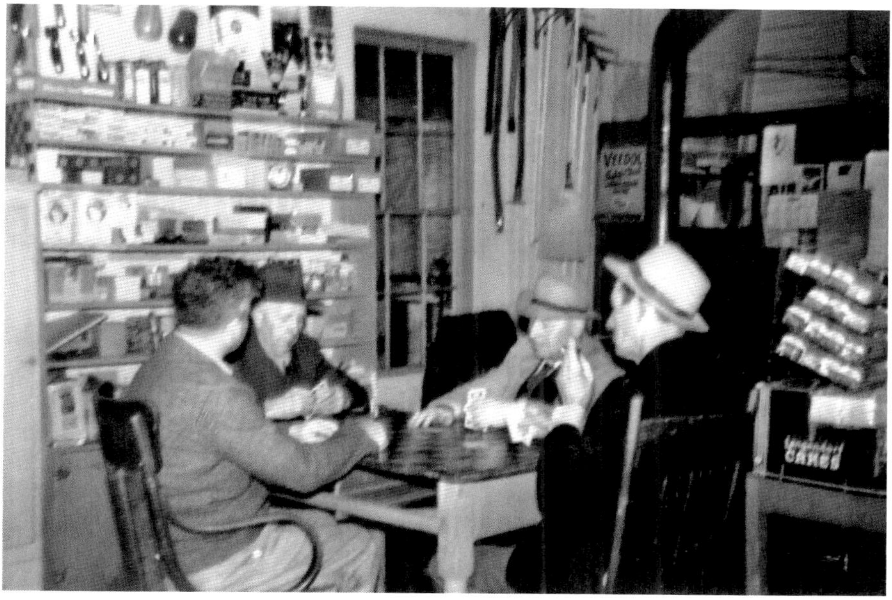

A rare picture of card players inside the San Ramon General Store, circa 1930. *Left to right*: Bill C. Fereira, Bill Johnson, Bill Meese and George Wood. *Museum of the San Ramon Valley.*

In 1946, the young Bill Fereira brought home a Chicago-raised bride, Violet Krga, for whom rural life was a shock. She said, "I couldn't get over how the ranchers were always talking about rain" and the fact that there were cattle everywhere. For Bill, there was no place like home. "This is where I grew up. I never thought to leave it." He opened a garage and repair shop right next to his father's general store, served as a volunteer fireman in Danville and later became San Ramon's fire chief.

Several people remember the gypsies who traveled through the valley picking walnuts and doing odd jobs. In 1977, Bill Fereira said, "There were lots of gypsies. They'd come into the general store and stuff things down their clothes." Some of them spoke Serbian among themselves, and Violet Fereira could understand them.

Across the street from the general store, several businesses were built. The Eight to Five Club (the Brass Door after 1955) featured steam beer and nickel slot machines.

In the decades from 1940 to 1970, the nine-county Bay Area's population tripled. The San Ramon Valley began to grow when Aerojet-General

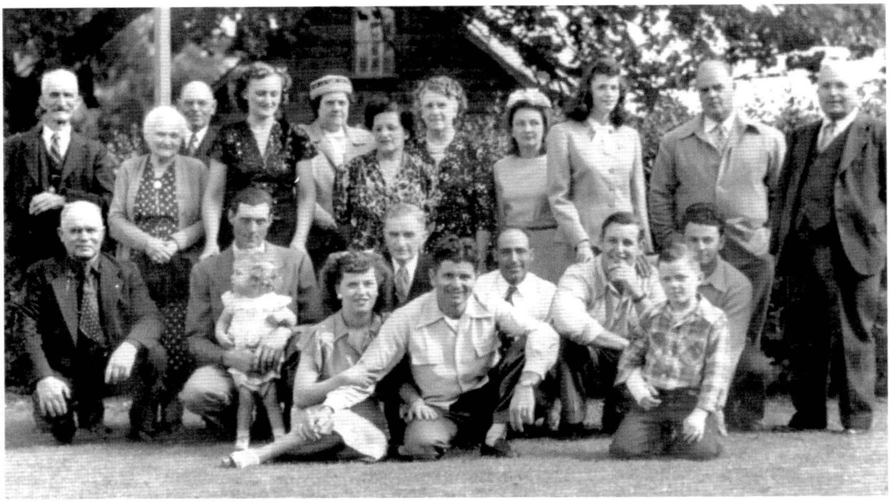

Bill Fereira introduced his new bride, Violet Krga Fereira, to his hometown friends at a party on April 26, 1946. Greeting them in the first row are (left to right) Violet and Bill Fereira and young Gordon Beatty; second row: Leo Norris III, Howard Wiedemann holding daughter Roxanne, Noel Norris, Tiny Peters, Robert Todoroff and Wilbert Sousa; third row: George Norris, Grace Norris, Everett Lynch, Doris Wiedemann, Mattie Wiedemann, Virgie Peters, Ramona (Lynch) Read, Mrs. Beatty, Susan Todoroff, Newell Beatty and Joe Lawrence. *Museum of the San Ramon Valley.*

Nucleonics brought seven hundred jobs to San Ramon in the early sixties. A steady row of cars droned down the old highway with locals dubbing it "gasoline alley." Everyone welcomed the interstate freeway that opened through San Ramon in late 1966.

Hundreds of new homes were built, and these new populations wanted more schools and parks, more police, senior services and local entertainment. The Golden Skate brought roller-skating to San Ramon in 1975. People went to eat at Villa San Ramon and the Brass Door in the old village. The fifty-year-old San Ramon Hall on Old Crow Canyon Road became the Valley Playhouse.

In the '60s, the San Ramon Homeowners Association organized to represent residents at Contra Costa County meetings and the Dublin San Ramon Services District board. The Greater San Ramon Improvement Association and San Ramon Valley Chamber of Commerce planning committee weighed in on growth proposals from a business perspective.

The 1965 chamber of commerce brochure lauded the area as "a valley that offers gracious living—prestige homes—the best weather in the Bay

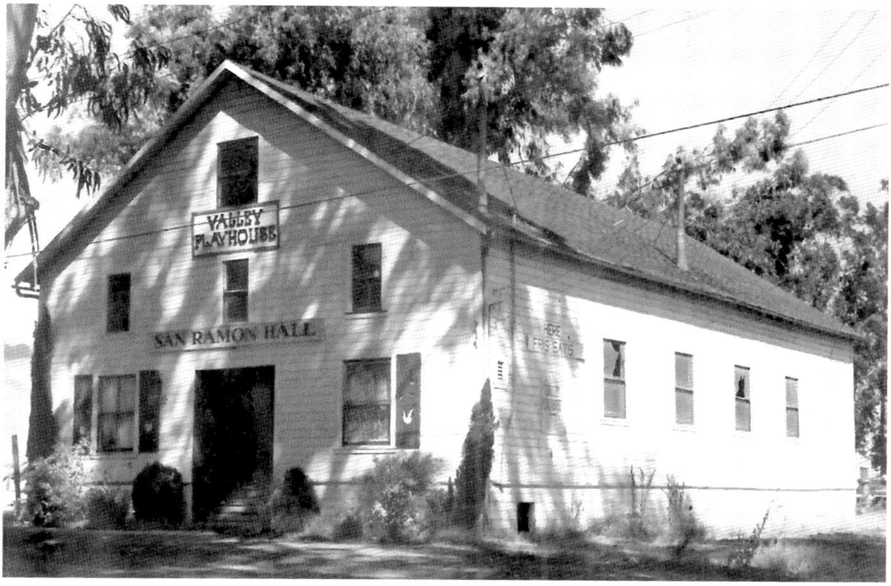

San Ramon Hall became the popular Valley Playhouse in the 1960s. *Museum of the San Ramon Valley.*

Area—walnut-studded countryside, within minutes of the major metropolitan centers. All nestled within the shadow of historic Mount Diablo."

Tony Dehaesus, the county's planning director, promoted a new type of zoning to provide community facilities and parks, the Planned Unit Development (PUD). He said that, in negotiations with homebuilders, the county lacked a mechanism to provide such requirements. After much debate, the board of supervisors adopted the PUD as a planning option in 1963. Housing developers began to create parks, pools and trails along with homes; Greenbrook Homes and Inverness Park were early examples.

Schools were crammed as young families moved in. The new San Ramon Elementary School, which had opened in 1950, couldn't handle the influx. Classes went into portables and had double sessions. The most unusual new school opening occurred in 1969 when Neil Armstrong Elementary put student classes into newly constructed homes during the autumn term while the school building was completed.

The Dublin San Ramon Services District purchased six acres for a park east of Alcosta Boulevard with a red barn and house on the site. After Proposition 13 passed in 1978 reducing the district's programming funds, San Ramon residents organized a board and leased the buildings.

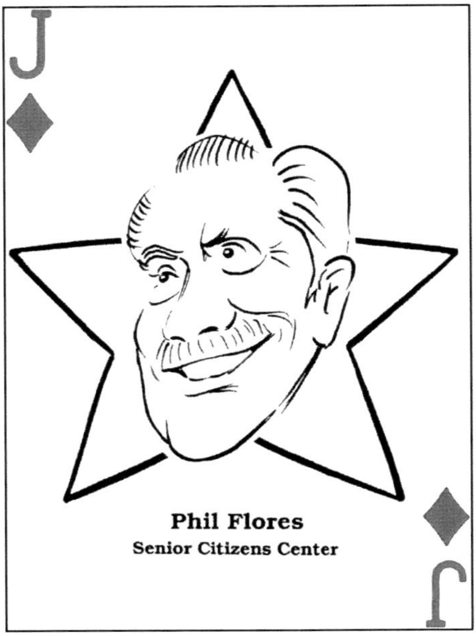

Phil Flores on a playing card, 1988. *Museum of the San Ramon Valley.*

An extraordinary volunteer effort spearheaded by the energetic Diane Schinnerer and senior Phil Flores provided a drop-in center for seniors in the newly named White House. There were bingo games, baking classes, tax classes, dances and much more. A Red Barn Arts group headed by Sally Scholl put on memorable annual Wild West fundraisers to support the programs.

The freeway cut through the eastern part of San Ramon's historic village, and when the Crow Canyon Road interchange swung west, it altered the old highway, razed the historic Thorup House and eliminated Lynch Road. From a 1950 population of 4,630, the entire San Ramon Valley grew to 57,307 in 1980.

The San Ramon Fire District began in 1963 to cope with the growth. Some new houses had no telephones for six months. Distant from the county seat in Martinez, law enforcement by the sheriff was practically nonexistent. In the early '70s, Mary Lou Oliver called 911 about a pipe bomb at Twin Creeks Elementary School, and it took police one hour and forty-five minutes to get there.

All this development meant the end of agriculture in San Ramon. One rancher, Jerry Henry, said flat out: "I hate development. I really do." He grew up helping his father A.W. Henry with Angus cattle on the Diamond Welford three-hundred-acre ranch east of the old highway and then began his own Bar JH Ranch on the west side. "This was a beautiful valley before the city allowed all these developments," pointing to the new homes just across from his ranch between Westside Drive and Pine Valley Road.

Not long after San Ramon incorporated in 1983, the first mayor, Diane Schinnerer, said in a *Oakland Tribune* article: "This is the most affluent cultural wasteland in the area. We lack facilities most other cities have including parks, a community college, gymnasiums, libraries, a museum and community cultural center and recreational programs."

The Party Place

San Ramon Hall

Parties, dances and plays helped to break up the hard work and tedium of ranch life. In San Ramon, for over forty years, the gathering place was the 1867 San Ramon Grammar School. Strong farm boys removed the partition in the middle, desks were pushed to one side and folks partied on.

The only large place for a dance in the valley was the 1874 Grange Hall in Danville, and by the end of the century, it was showing its age.

In 1896, the *Contra Costa Gazette* announced the formation of a San Ramon Public Hall Association, with the specific goal of building a public hall. Minnie Lynch and Anita Glass were two who worked to raise funds for this building. Anita was president of the association, which sold stock for the hall's construction. Fundraisers of all sorts were sponsored and supported by the community.

The San Ramon Hall was built by contractor Mr. Jensen in May 1911. By June, the building was in place, located along Old Crow Canyon Road just west of the old highway. The *Gazette* covered summer events at the hall in nearly every issue. One Saturday night dance, sponsored by the "Lady Boosters" was reported in the *Gazette*: "A great deal of merriment was had by the raffling off of a sheep donated by the Bishop Ranch to benefit the new hall." On July 8, 1911, a grand ball for over one hundred couples was held there. Mabel Christensen's orchestra provided music for many of the entertainments.

On December 2, 1911, the *Contra Costa Gazette* again took notice: "The shareholders deserve much credit for the way they are improving their

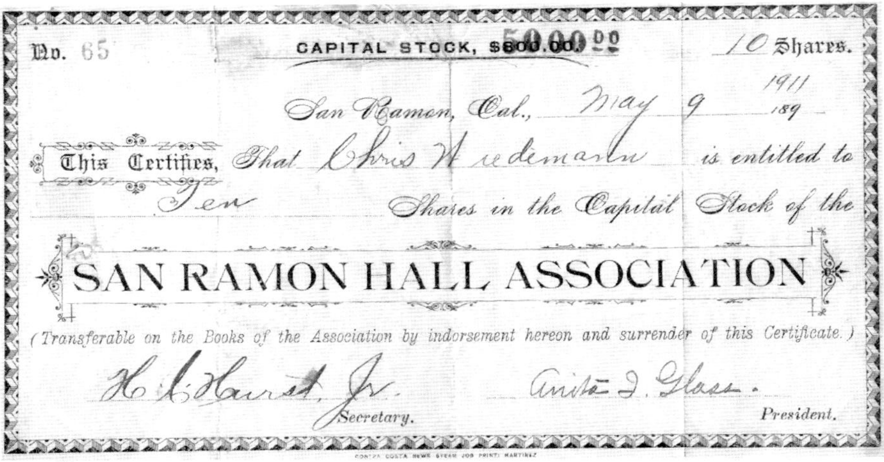

No. 65 CAPITAL STOCK, $500.00 10 Shares.

San Ramon, Cal., May 9 1911

This Certifies, That Chris Wiedemann is entitled to Ten Shares in the Capital Stock of the

SAN RAMON HALL ASSOCIATION

(Transferable on the Books of the Association by indorsement hereon and surrender of this Certificate.)

H. C. Hurst Jr. Secretary. Anita I. Glass. President.

This San Ramon Hall Association receipt showed that Chris Wiedemann had purchased ten shares in the hall. Signed by H.C. Hurst and Anita I. Glass, these shares were used to fundraise for the new building. Dated May 9, 1911. *Museum of the San Ramon Valley.*

hall, making it one of the most attractive places for public gatherings in this vicinity."

The December 23, 1911 *Contra Costa Gazette* wrote:

> *The residents of San Ramon never appreciated their new hall more than they did on last Friday night at their entertainment and dance. Heretofore the school house had to be cleared before the entertainment to prepare for the dance and as there is always large crowd at these affairs it was a very hard and unsatisfactory task. This year at the close of the* [school] *exercise those wishing to remain had only to walk a few steps from the school house to the hall where refreshments were served and dancing continued the rest of the night.*

Newspapers reported political speeches, graduations, May Day celebrations, musicals, plays and dances at the building. Henry Wiedemann told about balls that went on all night with a break for a midnight supper, especially during the Christmas season. Some parties were masquerades with lavish costumes and the dramatic removal of masks at midnight.

In the '20s, dances were sponsored by such groups as the Companions of Foresters, the Royal Neighbors of America and the Liberty Club, all providing a live orchestra for a usually one-dollar admission.

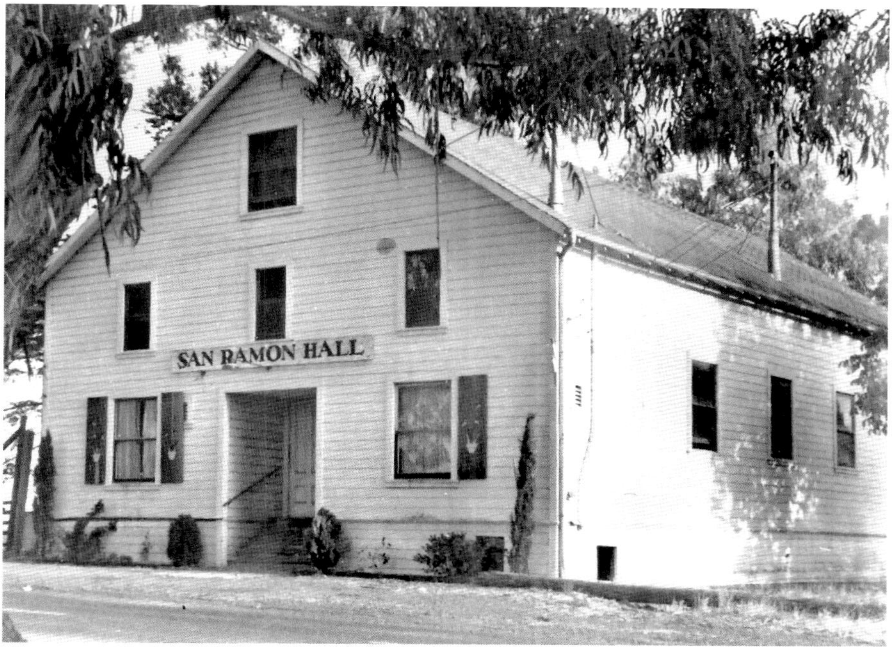

A picture of the San Ramon Hall on Old Crow Canyon Road about 1940. *Museum of the San Ramon Valley.*

In 1939, Carmen Geldermann, granddaughter of Joel and Minerva Harlan, recalled "dances where the wail of many babies in the cloakroom at times drowned out the fiddles." Young couples tucked their babies in the cloakroom for the night and danced 'til dawn, so they could see on the drive home.

Regular Saturday night dances rotated through the Tri-Valley. In the 1930s, the first weekly Saturday night party was at the Legion Hall in Danville, the second and fourth in Livermore and the third at the San Ramon Hall.

The 1941 *Walnut Kernel* described these dances: "On the first Saturday night of each month, the post and women's auxiliary have an oldtime dance where middle-aged folk may enjoy the polka, schottische, mazurka, Danish polka, Tye waltz, two-step, three-step, quadrille, lancers and other dances they learned when they were children."

Roxanne Lindsay recalls as a girl standing on the balcony and watching the band on stage and the dancers. It was an exciting place for small children. Bill Fereira said, "We used to drag hay around the floor to polish it for some rip snortin' dancing including the schottische and polka."

The building morphed into the Valley Playhouse in the 1960s. Advertised as Little Theatre Entertainment, it featured amateur actors called the Valley Players. Howard Wiedemann was one of the actors. Some of the plays were *Destry Rides Again*, *Picnic* and *Bell Book and Candle*.

As with other buildings in the village, the hall was razed in the 1960s.

Rose Peters Emery's Recollections

When she was ninety-seven, Rose Peters Emery wrote a memorable book, *Footprints in the Soil, a Portuguese-Californian Remembers*, which chronicled her life growing up on Peters Ranch, north of San Ramon Village. She and her siblings walked just under a mile to San Ramon Grammar School, which she entered in 1911. She drew a picture of the 1916 community as she recalled it.

On pages 101–102, she described the village:

> *The village of San Ramon was then very small. As I remember it, clustered together near the corner of the Danville–San Ramon Road* [now San Ramon Valley Boulevard] *and the old Crow Canyon Road to the north of Bollinger Creek were Hurst's store and post office, the Community Hall, Olsson's blacksmith shop and the jail, or calaboose as it was always called, a word derived from the Spanish* calaboso. *The latter was always empty though in earlier days it may have housed an occasional drunk. Then, south of the bridge over the creek, there were a saloon and Thorup's shoemaker shop plus a scattering of houses. That was it.*

The Peters family lived on the old highway, making it easy for peddlers to reach them. Although the family raised their own chickens and several milk cows and grew vegetables, traveling vendors brought a variety of welcome items to ranch homes.

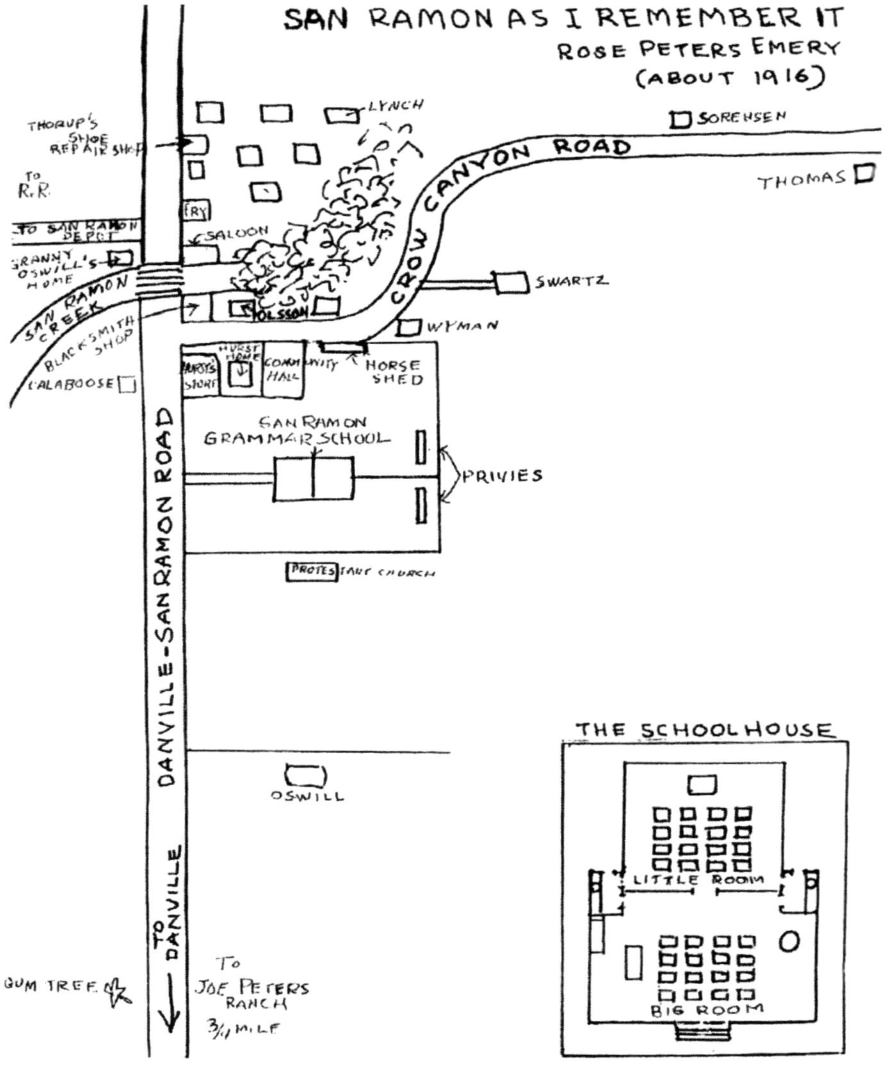

Rose Peters Emery made this drawing of the San Ramon village as she remembered it in 1916. She started grammar school in 1911. *Museum of the San Ramon Valley.*

Mrs. Emery wrote on pages 136–137:

> *The meat, fish and vegetable men visited us weekly. One woman regularly walked the entire four miles from Danville carrying a huge nesting basket*

that must have weighed fifty pounds…She would take them apart on our kitchen floor to display her wares, which included sewing notions like needles, safety pins, buttons…and personal items like hairpins, combs and shoelaces.

A tinsmith came by and mended tin pans for Mama…The Watkins man made regular calls. From him Mama would buy a big bottle of vanilla and liniment she like to use on her hip. A five-inch can of Carbo salve was also a must—said to contain carbolic acid guaranteed to work as well for horses' galled shoulders as for our own cuts and bruises.

Sometimes the family sold their own products. "Now and then a chicken man would come to buy a few of Mama's chickens. He would pack them in with others in a coop in the back of his wagon. 'Aren't you afraid they'll die?' Mama asked. 'Sometimes they do,' he replied, 'But they're good enough for tamales.'"

So much of the Peters family's story reflects the Portuguese American experience. Jose Pires Azevedo, renamed with Peters as a last name, came as an immigrant and never learned to read and write. But he worked hard and intelligently to become a successful rancher. His second wife, Rose Lawrence, was born in Tassajara Valley east of San Ramon. With her grammar school education and smarts, she assisted him in the ranch business. Mrs. Peters helped three of their children became University of California graduates. One son, Ed, became the first Portuguese American marine brigadier general. Danville's main store, Freitas and Peters, was run for years by her stepson Frank.

Rose Emery first saw the Danville Ranch housing development that covers much of the Peters Ranch today when she was in her nineties. In her book's conclusion, she wrote:

No farmer will ever again take a crop from that fertile land where once stood great stacks of baled hay and neatly piled sacks of wheat. No sleek red cattle will feed our growing population. I closed my eyes to blot out the changes. I want to remember my family's farm as it was in 1915, a place of beauty, serenity and productive work, a varied playground for growing children.

*I am 97 years old now and I am the only one left of my childhood family…I have managed to keep my independence. Yet I know I'll never get over that feeling of loss and nostalgia—*saudades, *the Portuguese call it—for my childhood family and our beautiful land.*

Libraries, Past and Present

A traditional community library provides books for people to take home and read. In the nineteenth century, having access to a library meant people could learn about the world beyond school, neighbor conversations, occasional newspapers or lectures. In San Ramon's early years, the only books that existed were in private homes.

Rose Peters Emery wrote that there was no library at the San Ramon Grammar School, not even a few books, when she began school in 1911. She recalled a teacher reading a book a chapter at a time. "For children with no radio, television, movies or storybooks it was as exciting as a Saturday matinee cliffhanger." She also commented, "Reading was not a possible amusement for us because, except for the Sears and Roebuck catalogue, there were no books in our house."

From 1903 to 1911 California's State Library had a Traveling Book Service that loaned fifty books to different communities for three months. The Danville Grange applied for this service in 1906. Early in 1910, Mary More was appointed assistant librarian and took charge of the newly arrived books.

In 1911, the state legislature enabled counties to establish public library service in unincorporated areas. The Grange endorsed the idea of a County Free Library in 1913, and on November 9, 1913, the Danville branch of the new county library opened with 104 books. They were available at the Danville Improvement Club on Front Street.

In 1925, Edith Clark became Danville's librarian, and the following year, the library moved to the new Legion Hall, at the corner of Prospect and

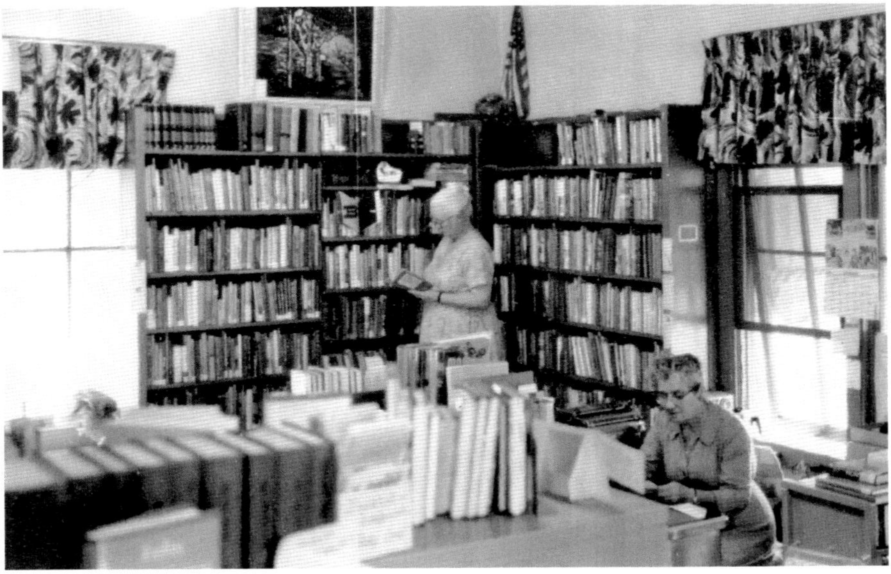

This rare photograph shows the library at the American Legion Hall in Danville, today called the Veterans Hall. Librarians Grace Warren (standing) and Myrtle Osborn are shown at work. *Contra Costa County Library.*

Hartz Avenues. According to the April 1926 *News Notes of California Libraries*, "The room is a joy to the whole community. On March 15 and 16, a force from the county library moved the books...The library was opened the next day without ceremony. The part of the building devoted to the library is very delightful, sunny and large enough for a few years."

San Ramon's library began in 1919 at the San Ramon Grammar School and continued in a San Ramon store owned by Annie L. Fry. After Fry died, in 1929, a Mrs. DuBois ran the library for two years. For a time, the library was housed in Mrs. Victoria Soto's home in a bookcase that her son Bill still possesses. Ann Wiedemann Kaplan remembers the Soto library at the corner of Thorup Lane and today's San Ramon Valley Boulevard: "She had a couple hundred books in her living room and she let people check them out." It was a very small town then.

The county's library history indicates that the San Ramon Library ended in 1933, with the supposition that readers were using the Legion Hall books.

At the Legion Hall, Edith Clark was librarian for twenty years, followed by Myrtle Osborn (1945) and Grace Warren (1956) with Mrs. Osborn continuing as assistant for many years. Young Winky Camacho worked part time at this library in 1956 and said it was a tiny room with storage in the bathroom. Mrs. Warren got boxes from Elliott's Bar and used them for book storage. Gary Soto and Barbara Park recall this library and the stereopticon on one table—an early form of multimedia.

In the '50s, a San Ramon Valley Library League lobbied for a new library, which was built in Danville and opened on June 12, 1961. Called "space age" in design, it was modern, with soaring glass windows at one end and a second floor. Its customers came from the whole valley.

San Ramon was starting to grow, and in 1974, the San Ramon Homeowners Association set up a survey to see if the community wanted a library. Mike Wahlig, who was president, said, "There was just no interest. Everyone here goes to the Dublin library." There was also a Dublin Library bookmobile. In the *Tri-Valley News*, the head of the Contra Costa library system, Clarence Waters, said the effort was probably "a bit premature."

However, with incorporation in 1983, there was a groundswell of support for a new San Ramon library. Daniel Hancock of Shapell Industries volunteered to donate $100 per home for each of the 837 homes in their Newcastle development and start a San Ramon Library fund. He said, "We can plant a seed and hopefully it will come to fruition."

A San Ramon Library Foundation was formed in 1985 to receive these and other donated funds. Its first board of directors was a who's who of leaders for the new city, including realtor Juanita Whitney, Daniel Hancock of Shapell, Alex Mehran from Sunset Development Company, council member Diane Schinnerer, rancher Jeff Wiedemann, Lois Farness (San Ramon AAUW President) and attorney Cynthia Hannon.

The city issued Certificates of Participation, the county agreed to provide operating funds, land was deeded (in lieu of park fees) and some construction was paid for by Pacific Rim Development Company. Many developers, nonprofits and individuals contributed. Co-chaired by Diane Schinnerer and Lois Farness, an intensive campaign to buy books for the library successfully raised $500,000 for thirty thousand new books.

San Ramon opened its new library at 100 Montgomery Road on April 15, 1989, just six years after the community incorporated. Designed by Clifford Moles, Associates, AIA, the building was 18,238 square feet in size with room for fifty-five thousand volumes. Library volunteers were recruited outside four supermarkets for two days just before the opening. The city and foundation threw a three-day celebration with parties and special events for children. The new library represented a huge community effort and symbolized the quality of facilities the city council wanted to provide.

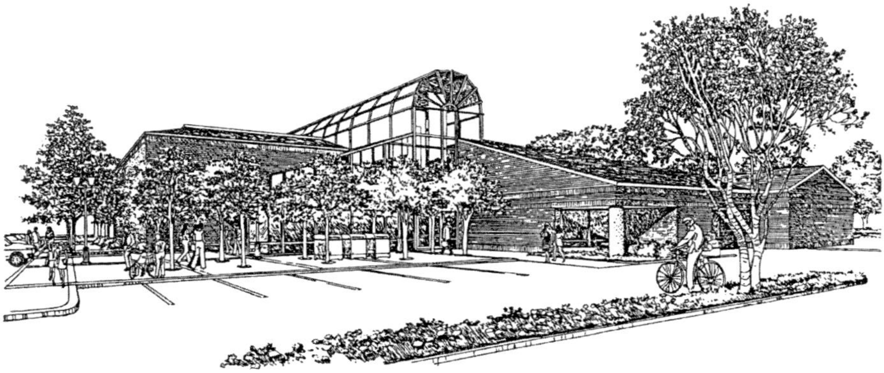

Architectural drawing of the San Ramon main library, designed in 1987 by Clifford Moles. The library opened in 1989. *Museum of the San Ramon Valley.*

Dougherty Station Library opened in 2005. This photograph shows its western entrance ten years later. *Museum of the San Ramon Valley.*

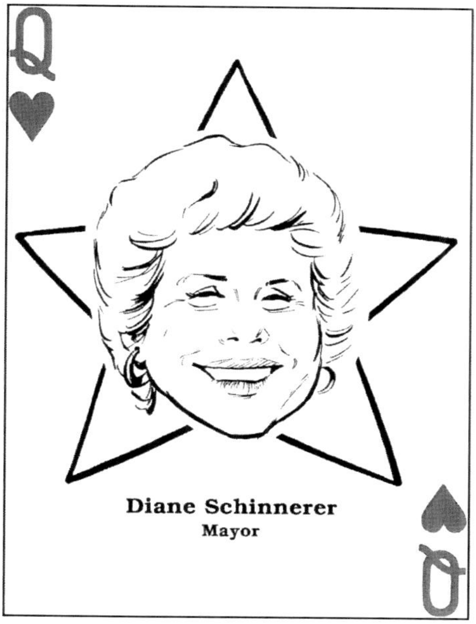

Mayor Diane Schinnerer on a playing card, 1988. *Museum of the San Ramon Valley.*

It became the center of activities for much of the community, drawing people to hear speakers, view exhibits and use the Internet. A jazz festival began in 1996 and has grown exponentially each year. Joyce Gunn was the energetic branch manager from 1991 to 2006.

San Ramon's council was not one to accept status quo in anything, including library services. They discussed setting up a library independent of the county but rejected the idea. In addition, they added funds for staffing and open hours, so that the library was open more days and longer hours than the county could provide.

The libraries are well used by students, especially Iron Horse Middle School students, who take a short walk to the main branch. One possible result of this use: teens accounted for more than 36 percent of the library's 8,600 volunteer hours in 2014.

In 2005, a second facility, the Dougherty Station Library, opened to help serve the growing Dougherty Valley and the San Ramon campus of Diablo Valley College. This library was the county library's first joint use facility. With its name, it commemorates James Witt Dougherty, who had purchased much of the Amador Rancho land so many years ago.

And what of the San Ramon Library's future? As part of city center plans for 2015–17, the main library will be expanded to 21,520 square feet and reconfigured to fit modern library uses. A new entry will face north toward the modern city hall with a second entry from the parking lot. ATI Architects & Engineers are providing the design.

The library's stated mission is to be a vital and thriving community resource that serves the diverse informational and educational needs of the public and, in the Dougherty Valley, the needs of the Diablo Valley Community College San Ramon campus students. Remarkably, 43,629 San Ramon residents hold a Contra Costa County Library card out of a 2015 population of over 78,000.

San Ramon Welcomes the Freeway in 1966

By the '50s, the old highway was jammed with cars bumper to bumper, and people were eager to welcome the proposed interstate freeway through the San Ramon Valley. But where to put it, exactly?

Meetings attended by 200 or more residents focused on the freeway location in Danville and San Ramon. These were large meetings considering that the whole valley had a population of just 12,700 people in 1960.

The main options were an eastern route versus a mid-valley route. Both generated controversy. The September 19, 1962 *Valley Pioneer* said that the county proposals were "causing havoc in the area." There were homes and businesses in the mid-valley area that would be displaced. The eastern route would have gone through open ranchland until it reached the modern Aerojet-General plant in north San Ramon. The valley's largest employer (seven hundred employees in 1963), Aerojet resisted that route, and with its clout as a government contractor, the mid-valley route was chosen.

In the early 1960s, county planners worked with the Greater San Ramon Improvement Association to generate a master plan for the area that anticipated freeway-generated growth. The association's goal was "to aid and direct the development and progress of the greater San Ramon area." Some new enterprises were already in place in San Ramon, including Aerojet, Filper (fruit processing equipment) and the Cryodry Corporation (microwave heating systems).

County planners made it clear that they thought the old buildings in San Ramon Village were real eyesores. In that era, saving historic buildings wasn't usually considered. In 1963, the San Ramon Fire District even burned down the classic San Ramon General Store as practice for their fire fighters.

Russ Griffith, principal planner for the county planning department, suggested that in San Ramon the new freeway should demolish the buildings east of the old highway, including the Brass Door restaurant and bar, San Ramon Motors, San Ramon Realty and the A&W Root Beer restaurant. He reasoned that San Ramon's downtown could have a new start. Up-to-date buildings were in vogue, such as Concord's Sunvalley Mall, which was scheduled to open in 1967.

Congressman John Baldwin was very much involved in the right-of-way discussions. Baldwin's campaign committee came to the Brass Door after meetings, and of course, the owner let them know that he objected to Griffith's draconian suggestion. One local story says Baldwin made a call directly from the restaurant reminding transportation staff that federal funds were building the freeway and that Baldwin was the contact for those funds. As a result, the freeway avoided the Brass Door but still clipped off the end of the building just south of the restaurant.

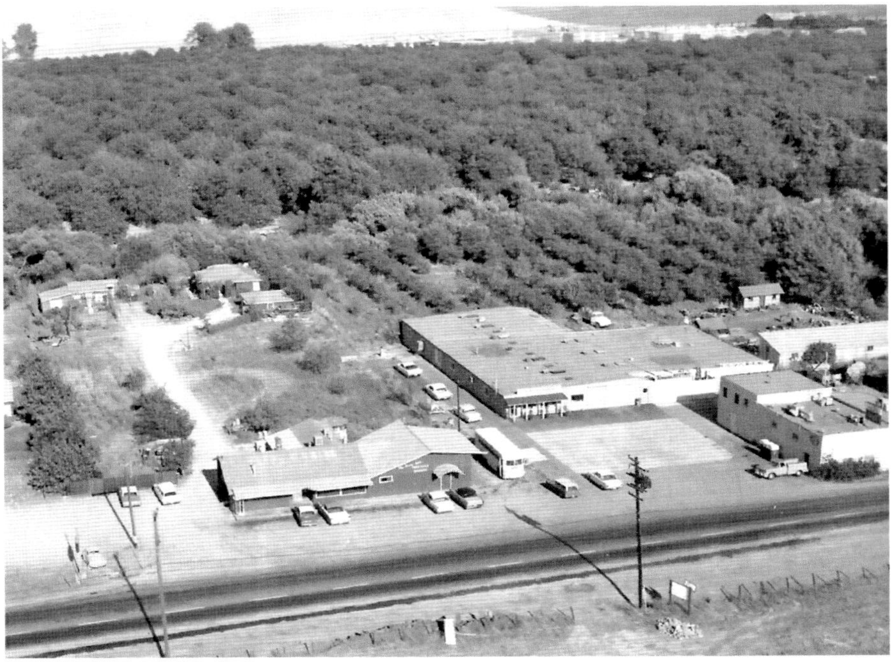

This aerial photograph shows the Brass Door in the center with nothing but orchards to the east. The I-680 freeway is now right next to the restaurant's parking lot. *Museum of the San Ramon Valley.*

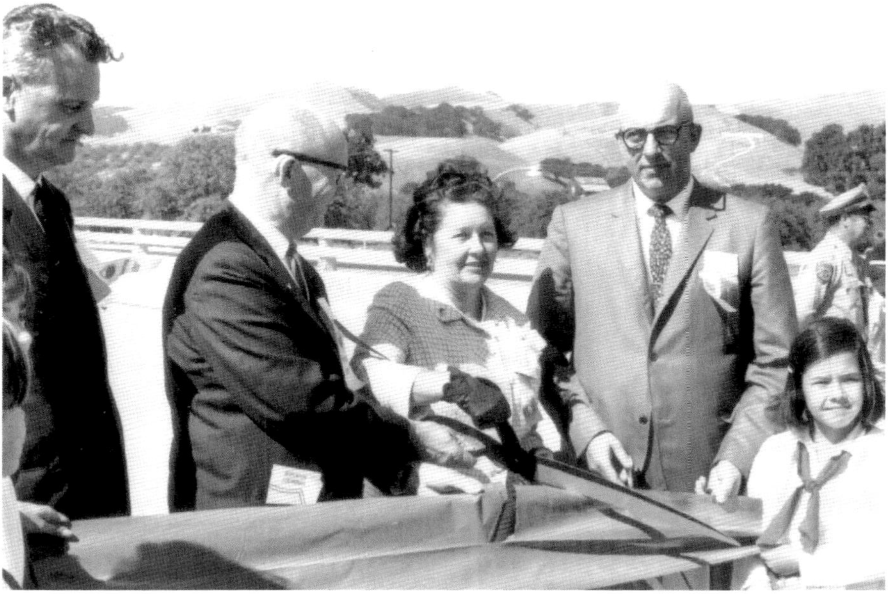

The I-680 freeway opened in October 1966 and was celebrated as DD Day (Danville to Dublin). Here is the ribbon cutting, which took place at the Crow Canyon Overcrossing. *From left to right*: historian Wilson Close, district engineer Alan S. Hart, Mrs. Hart, chamber of commerce president Al Kaplan and a child. *Museum of the San Ramon Valley.*

Initial off-ramp plans did not include one in San Ramon at all. After lobbying by Howard Wiedemann and others, the Crow Canyon Road off-ramp was included. Its off-ramps realigned the old highway to the west, and the historic Thorup House was razed in the process. Norris and Bollinger Canyon Roads had only freeway overpasses.

The I-680 freeway opened its Walnut Creek to Danville section through the valley and ended at Sycamore Valley Road in 1964. The next 5.9-mile section went south through San Ramon and was built by Frederickson and Watson from 1965 to 1966.

Al Kaplan was president of the San Ramon Valley Chamber of Commerce at the time. He later recalled the modern equipment used on the freeway and off-ramp installations.

On September 24, 1966, "DD I-680 Days" celebrated the freeway linkage between Danville and Dublin through San Ramon. Historian Wilson Close headed the "DD Freeway Celebration," which included an antique car parade. Pioneer descendants Matilda Elliott, Friederiche

Jackson and Leo Norris were in the first car. Other dignitaries included the new congressman Jerry Waldie, state senator George Miller Jr. and county supervisor James Moriarity.

But what changes the freeway brought! No more cars end-to-end throughout the valley, and people could easily make turns on the old highway. The relief from congestion gave local leaders hope that there might be fewer gas stations along the road.

Peace and quiet along the boulevard was the best benefit. John May walked out to get the newspaper one morning after the freeway opened in Danville and saw no cars at all on the old highway. When he came back to the house, he said, "Margaret, it is as if a bomb dropped somewhere and we are the only people on earth."

With the Danville–San Ramon–Dublin link completed, the "DD 680" brochure bragged that motorists could completely circle the entire East Bay area in a seventy-three-mile loop without having to stop for one traffic signal. There were congratulations all round.

San Ramon's Fire Protection District, 1963–80

The year 1963 was a milestone for the history of firefighting in San Ramon. Growth was in the air as the new Aerojet-General plant expanded to nearly one thousand workers, agricultural land was being eyed for development and the I-680 freeway alignment was in place.

San Ramon was part of the huge East Contra Costa County Fire Protection District, while a Danville Fire District covered the northern part of the valley. Bill Fereira and Howard Wiedemann looked at the growing San Ramon area and new business buildings. They agreed that East County Fire was inadequate to the task of San Ramon fire protection. Thus, the San Ramon Fire Protection District was born.

Bill and his two brothers had grown up in the little village of San Ramon where their father, William, owned the San Ramon General Store. Howard was a prominent rancher whose family had lived and ranched in San Ramon since the 1860s.

After the war, Fereira took fire science courses and became a Danville Fire District volunteer. Trained as a mechanic, he opened a garage next door to the general store. In the '50s, the East Contra Costa County Fire District ran San Ramon's fire service out of Fereira's garage, which housed the fire truck and jeep. He made a one-hundred-mile trip each month to service other fire trucks in the East County and answered fire calls twenty-four hours a day from a phone in his home. For these services, he was paid fifty dollars a month.

Fereira tells some colorful stories about the San Ramon Fire District's beginnings. He and Wiedemann talked to county supervisor Mel Nielsen

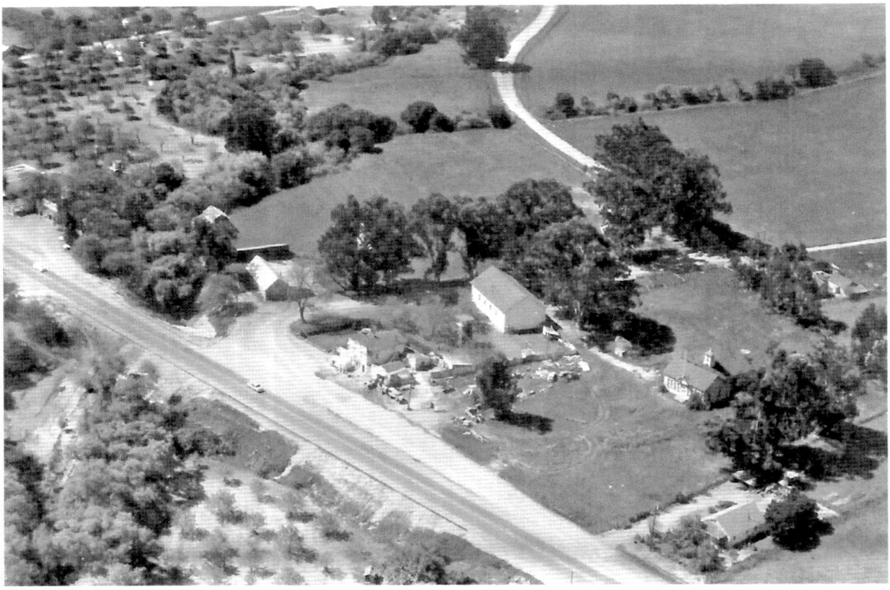

An aerial photograph shows the entire San Ramon village about 1955. *From left to right*: blacksmith shop, community hall, general store, garage and grammar school of San Ramon Village. *Museum of the San Ramon Valley.*

about a new San Ramon Fire District. Nielsen agreed but wanted it to be a dependent county fire district with a county-appointed commission and county-approved budget. The two San Ramon men wanted an independent district for San Ramon similar to Danville's. Independent districts had locally elected commissioners supported directly by the property tax. The County Board of Supervisors could make this decision.

A lawyer friend of Wiedemann's provided the county staff with a report for the supervisors that created such an independent district. Evidently, Nielsen didn't read the report carefully because the county supervisors voted to create an independent fire district for San Ramon on January 29, 1963.

When Nielsen found out, he was "hopping mad," according to Fereira. Nielsen tried unsuccessfully to rescind the vote. Then Chief Al Bates of the East County Fire Department swept in and took his district's fire equipment from San Ramon. Fereira said he began hiding the tools, including rakes, buckets and other items, but lost the truck to East County Fire. When Bates sent a man to take the fire siren down off its pole. Fereira got mad and threatened to shoot the guy down "like a jaybird." The siren was a former civil defense siren Bill had scrounged from San Francisco.

The first fire commissioners were Larry Davidson, Armand Borel, Mickey Schlesinger, Howard Wiedemann and A.C. "Johnny" Johnson. Schlesinger, a part owner of the Brass Door, bought a 1931 fire engine and placed it in front of the restaurant for the "Brass Door Volunteers." Fereira said that the district had really good fire commissioners. "They met in a tiny room and everybody smoked."

The district boundary was about twenty square miles, including Tassajara Valley to the east. It abutted the Danville district on the north and the Dublin San Ramon Services District on the south. About three hundred people lived in San Ramon in 1960. Fereira said, "It was all orchards then, different than today."

According to Fereira, there was no money for six months. The commissioners hired him as their first paid employee, making him a part-time captain for $300 a month while he continued to work at his garage. Bill borrowed a truck, recruited volunteers and answered calls twenty-four hours a day. Finally, on July 1, 1963, the new San Ramon Fire Protection District was able to tap a portion of the property tax and begin to acquire its own equipment. The district was on its way.

Bill Fereira became the full-time chief with one full-time fireman, Francis "Sunny" O'Shea. Fire suppression apparatus included a 750 GPM Van Pelt pumper, a 1,200-gallon capacity tanker (built by Fereira and the volunteers) and a pickup truck with extra equipment. San Ramon's first water mains and hydrants were installed in 1965. That year, seventy-five responses were made, most of which were fire calls.

Chief Fereira set up volunteer training twice a week that included drills and laying hose. In 1963, he organized a practice fire and burned down the San Ramon General Store, which was one of the oldest buildings in town. It happened this way: the older Fereiras had moved into a new house, and the store was left vacant. To be reoccupied, the store needed new wiring plus structural work, and the costs to bring it up to county code were prohibitive. So, it was burned to give the volunteers some actual experience. Nowadays, the historic store might have been saved, but in the '60s, the preservation movement was just beginning.

Many of the fires they fought were wild land fires. Lightning struck Mount Diablo's Eagle Peak area on August 1, 1977, and a memorable fire raged for five days. It topped the crest on the south side of the summit and eventually consumed 6,300 acres. Three local fire districts fought the flames together—Danville, San Ramon and Tassajara (organized in 1969)—and they used all the resources they could muster.

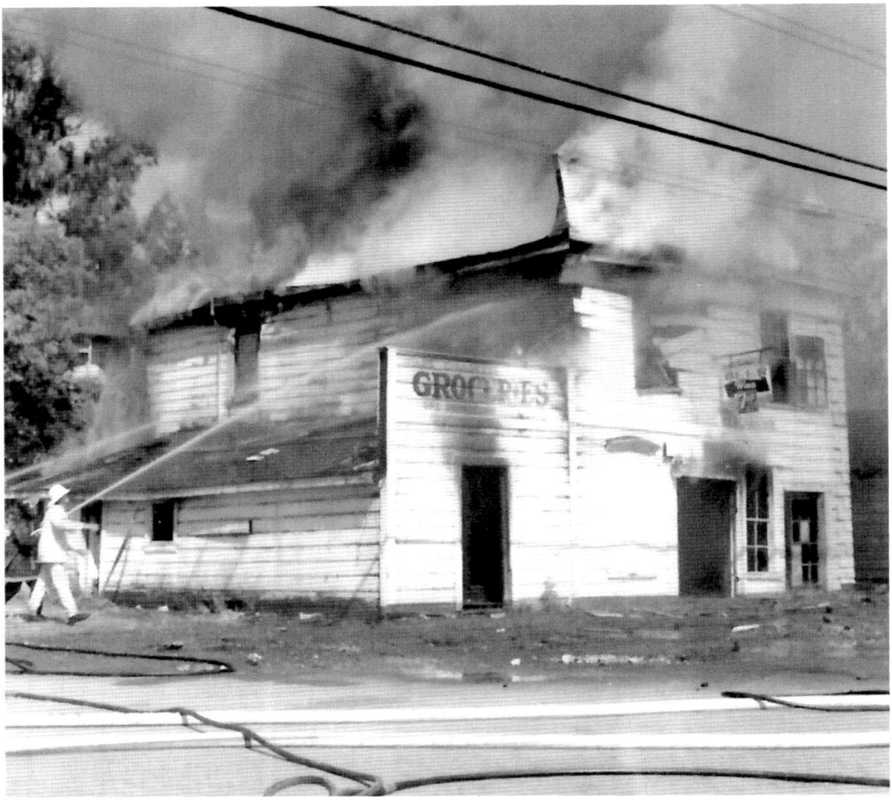

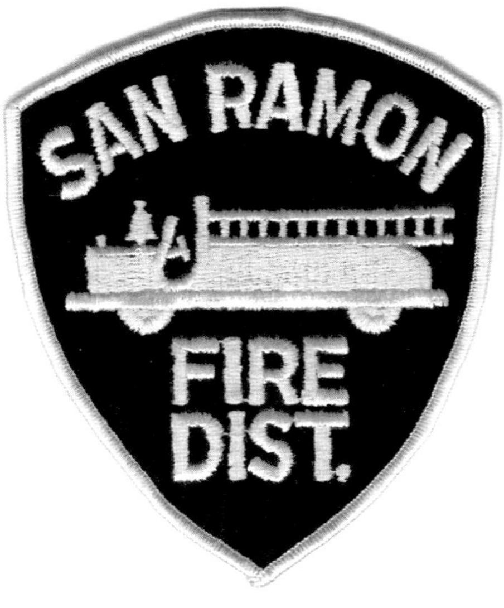

Above: The historic San Ramon General Store was burned down in 1963 so that San Ramon firefighters could practice their skills. *Museum of the San Ramon Valley.*

Left: This unique San Ramon Fire District patch was black with yellow lettering. It was designed by Chief Bill Fereira. *Museum of the San Ramon Valley.*

During the fiscal year 1975–76, the San Ramon department had 110 fire calls and 147 medical emergency calls. Because of the increase in medical calls, Chief Fereira said that "we bought a rescue vehicle because we were so remote from ambulance service. Some calls were taking too long." The firemen used the vehicle if the patient wasn't stable and contracted with an ambulance service out of Fremont for other transports. The nearest hospitals were Kaiser Permanente (nine miles away) and John Muir (eleven miles away), both in Walnut Creek.

The San Ramon trucks were bright yellow because a study in the '60s said that this color was the most visible under all conditions. The big "San Ramon Fire District" sign had a button that set off the siren. Fereira said that one day an older woman who was drunk pushed the siren button. She thought the fire station was a hotel. According to Fereira, fireman helped ranchers out when accidents happened, once removing a cow from a well and another time using two trucks to retrieve a horse from a creek.

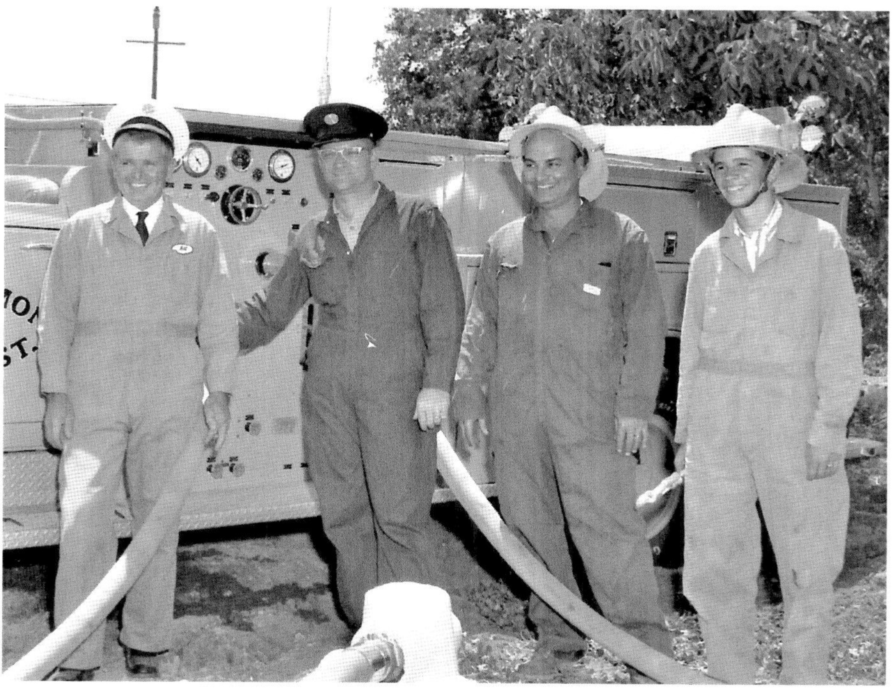

Standing in front of a yellow fire truck are (from left to right) fire chief Bill Fereira, Francis O'Shea, Don Warren and young Billy Fereira, shown about 1965. *Museum of the San Ramon Valley.*

Providing efficient fire service for the burgeoning population and new manufacturing buildings was a challenge. The whole valley had 2,120 people in 1940, 12,700 in 1960 and 57,307 in 1980. In the 1970s, Danville and San Ramon Fire District commissioners began contemplating a consolidation to create the San Ramon Valley Fire Protection District (SRVFPD).

There were serious concerns that the county's huge consolidated fire district would annex the two districts and reduce local fire services. In 1977, the county grand jury recommended that the San Ramon and Danville Fire Districts consolidate. Merger talks began in earnest after Proposition 13 passed.

Mel Deardorff, an assistant fire chief for Danville at the time, was very involved in the proposed merger. "Don Miladinovich was the spark plug for this merger, for sure. He was a board member for Danville Fire. He thought it made sense and was involved in a lot of behind-the-scenes politicking to make it happen…In 1978, Bill Fereira retired as chief in San Ramon, and he had really started that district. Bill was not happy about the prospect of a merger at first. It was hard for him to see the district change that way."

Fire district consolidation sparked huge debates throughout the community. A new Local Agency Formation Commission weighed in. The commission included city, county and public representatives and was committed to pursuing orderly growth. The valley's county supervisor Eric Hasseltine finally said, "Nowhere is provincialism more rampant than it is in the fire boards. You talk consolidation and they go nuts."

All agreed that a new district should be called the San Ramon Valley Fire Protection District. But there were differing opinions over emergency services, timing of the merger, who would be chief, firefighter seniority and retirement plans.

To make a really long story short, the two districts combined on March 18, 1980. Both boards endorsed consolidation unanimously, and the issue sailed through LAFCO hearings. By late spring, the new board included both San Ramon and Danville representatives Don Miladinovich, Lou Sylvia, Al Houvenin, Robert Ingram and Sam Pappalardo.

In the next decades, after much deliberation, the Tassajara Fire Protection District (1990) and the Dougherty Valley Regional Fire Authority (1997) joined as well. Today, the San Ramon Valley Fire Protection District is in place and provides a high level of fire protection for the entire valley.

Suburban San Ramon—South

The East Bay's inland valleys had been breadbaskets with cattle ranching on the hills for over a century. People discovered California during World War II and came to the Golden State in ever-increasing numbers. Interstate freeways facilitated suburban growth in the East Bay's agrarian valleys and a policy that taxed farmland for its potential use made change inevitable.

For years, a sign posted opposite the Brass Door announced, "San Ramon Pop. 100." The whole San Ramon Valley had only 2,000 people for most of the twentieth century. In the 1960 census, San Ramon did not appear at all. By 1970, the census listed "San Ramon Village" with a population of 4,084. This number reflected thousands of new homes in South San Ramon.

Developers Bob McLain and Ken Volk purchased 4,200 acres on both sides of the county line in the late 1950s. Realtor Harlan Geldermann (a descendant of San Ramon's Harlan family) assembled the parcels and sold them the agricultural land that stretched from around today's I-580 west to San Ramon Valley Road, north to Montevideo and east to Dougherty.

Lee Fereira heard about the Geldermann project and asked why anyone on earth would want to buy a house "in that swamp!" Indeed, marshes in Dublin and San Ramon were drained by Volk/McLain to enable the development.

Volk/McLain Communities Inc. proposed a new city with schools, shopping centers, church sites, a golf course, a hospital, library facilities, parks and a heliport. Experienced Southern California homebuilders,

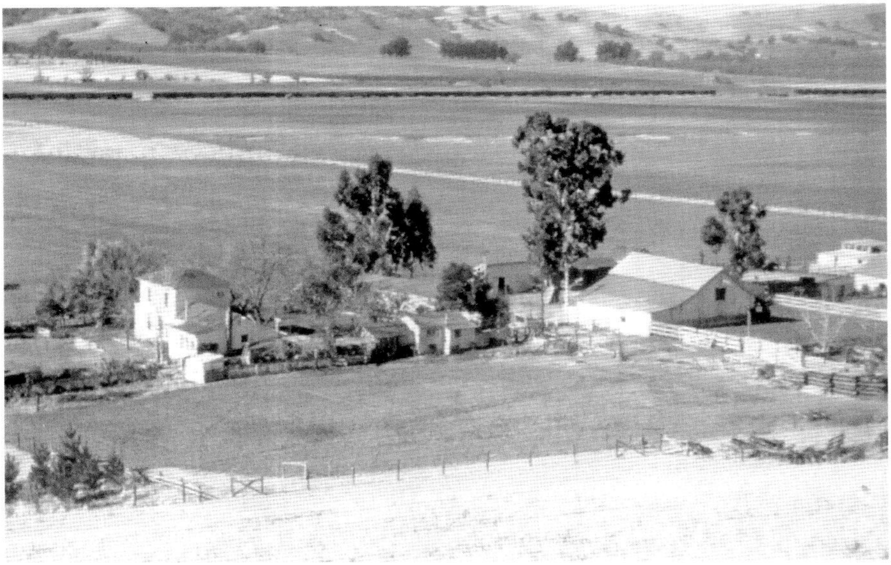

This view of A.W. Henry's Diamond Welford Ranch looks northwest across the valley about 1950. He raised Angus cattle. *Henry family collection.*

they planned 10,750 residences of varying types, from garden apartments to multifamily and single-family dwellings. And people came, lining up overnight to buy these starter homes and filling the schools beyond capacity. Houses went on the San Ramon market in 1961.

Dick and Joyce Fahey and their family moved to the first neighborhood on Balthusrol Court in June 1961. Twenty-five years later, Dick Fahey could still sing the Volk/McLain radio jingle: "Live in lovely San Ramon Village, City Close [cable bells ringing], Country Quiet [birds chirping]." Curious about the way government decisions would be made for his new home, he talked with Contra Costa County planning staff and soon became a spokesman for the new community, promoting parks and schools.

Of course, so many homes on agricultural land needed a complete new infrastructure of roads, water and sewer pipes. Volk and McLain turned to a small farmers' district that was named after the Dublin-area military base, Camp Parks. Created in 1953, the Parks Community Services District straddled the county line, covered 2,175 acres and focused on providing water and drainage for local farmers. The developers convinced the district's board to annex the property they had just purchased, which enlarged the district to 5,900 acres.

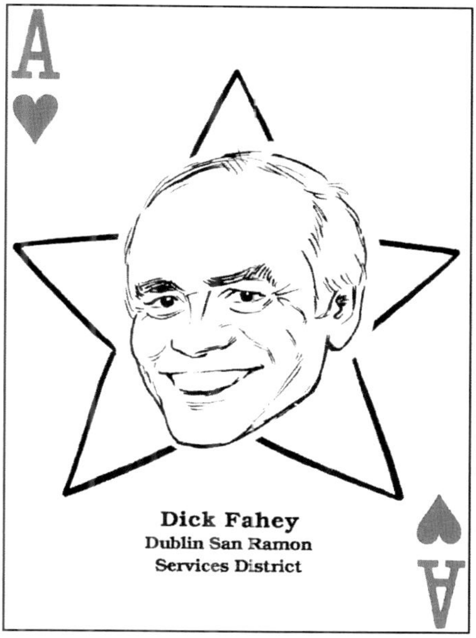

Richard Fahey on a playing card, 1988. *Museum of the San Ramon Valley.*

Renamed the Valley Community Services District (VCSD), the agency set about providing water, sewage treatment, garbage collection, fire protection, parks and recreation for the new residents. Alameda and Contra Costa County governments provided development approvals and police service, and the school districts in each county provided schools.

In 1962, shortly after people began moving in, residents organized the volunteer San Ramon Homeowners Association (SRHA) with Dick Fahey, Ed Lee and Chuck Henry taking the lead. In 1975, association president Mike Wahlig said, "We feel an obligation to look at them [new development proposals] because no one else here will."

The members of the SRHA provided an effective voice for the new homeowners and stuck their noses in everywhere. They commented on development proposals, promoted a successful vote to bring East Bay Municipal Utility District Sierra water to the area in 1967 and called for a San Ramon post office. They held builders accountable for what was promised, published a newsletter (typed by Joyce Wahlig), lobbied for schools and parks, sent members to local elected boards and planning commissions and commented on bus routes. Wahlig indicated that the county welcomed their input: "You ask for reasonable things, and you get reasonable answers."

VCSD was the only locally elected political show in town, and new residents vied for seats on the board in hotly contested elections. In 1966, Byron Athan was elected; in 1968, Dick Fahey, Tom Schweser and Ann Jolley defeated three of the incumbents. This new board led voters to pass a parks and recreation bond issue in 1972 to purchase land and construct recreation facilities and parks. Actual construction was slow in coming, so in 1975, urged on by the district's Park and Recreation Advisory Committee, led by Joe Covello and Ed Lee, the board authorized a 39 percent tax increase election to accelerate the construction schedule, provide maintenance and

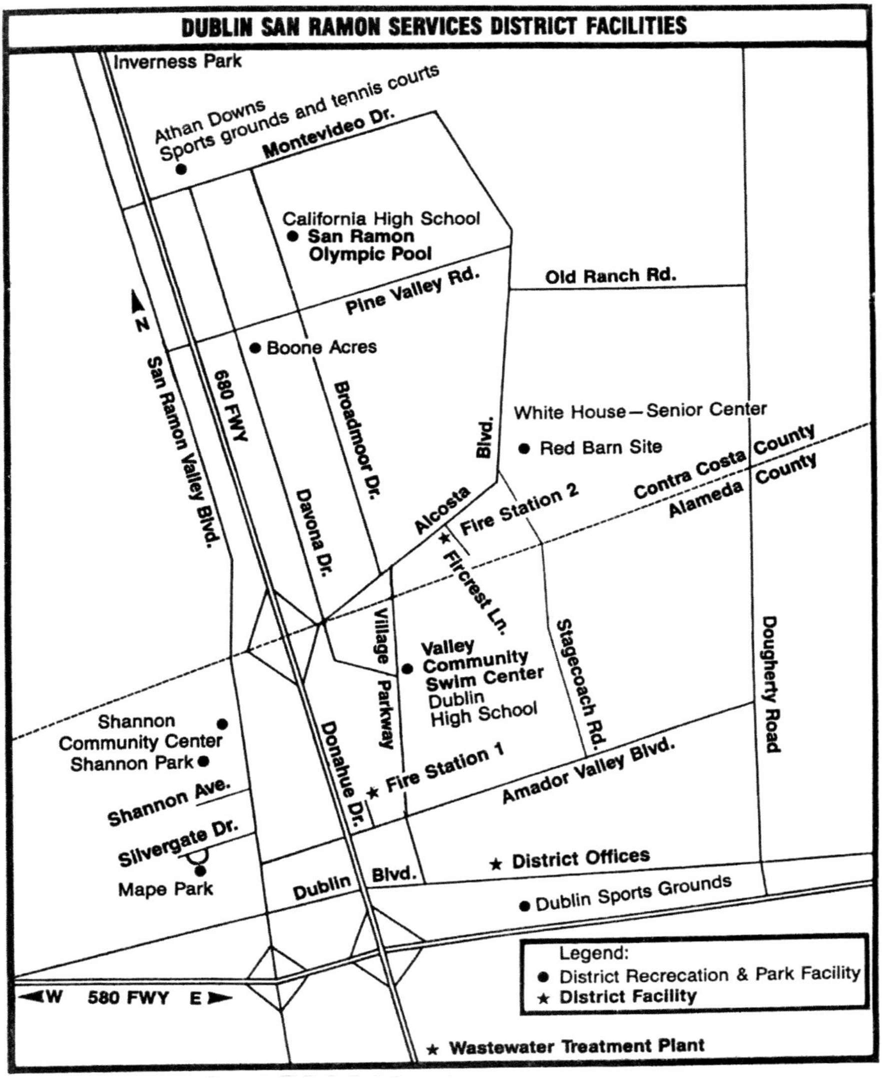

The Dublin San Ramon Services District included areas in both Contra Costa and Alameda Counties and provided a variety of services before San Ramon and Dublin were incorporated, circa 1980. *Museum of the San Ramon Valley.*

staff the facilities and parks. This latter general (nonspecific) tax increase election was overwhelmingly supported by San Ramon voters but, district-wide, passed by the razor-thin edge of thirty-eight votes. Joe Covello and Diane Schinnerer won board seats in 1977 and 1978.

In 1977, the district's name changed to Dublin San Ramon Services District (DSRSD), after some vigorous pro and con debates.

San Ramon homeowners also made sure that DSRSD bond issue projects were constructed as promised. For example, Ed Lee brought information about the Livermore Lab's Olympic pool management to DSRSD when the board was considering building a smaller pool at California High School as demanded by the school district. The Olympic-sized pool won out. One newspaper called the association "San Ramon's Unofficial Government."

California's Proposition 13 in 1978 put a cap on the property tax and caused a large decrease in funding for DSRSD's programs. The district sought new approaches to continue recreational services. Sports groups and new nonprofits leased the fields, provided maintenance (initially using home lawn mowers), raised sport club fees and created senior programs at the White House on Alcosta Boulevard using volunteers. DSRSD itself was able to survive financially due to its two-county district status and the legislative efforts of California state senator John Nejedly as well as frantic efforts by district board members and DSRSD fire chief Phil Phillips, who also served as the DSRSD financial officer.

Efforts to get more local control by incorporating a new city for the entire San Ramon Valley were voted on in 1967, 1973 and 1976. All failed, although San Ramon voters supported cityhood each time. Both Dick Fahey and Byron Athan ran for the proposed city council in 1967. George Filice, owner of San Ramon's Filper Corporation, ran as well, although he was opposed to incorporation. In 1979, a unique incorporation proposal across the county line that included both Dublin and San Ramon went to the voters. San Ramon rejected it decisively. One wag, Will Duberstein, took out a full-page ad that said, "If I wanted to live in Dublin I would have moved to Ireland."

Finally, San Ramon successfully incorporated in 1983 with overwhelming support.

The Schinnerers must have had animated dinner table conversations, as Diane became the first San Ramon mayor, and Don joined the DSRSD board in 1983. Livewire Joe Covello regularly pointed out that, while one school district covered the area, the new city had two fire districts, two garbage franchises, two park providers, two recreation programmers—even

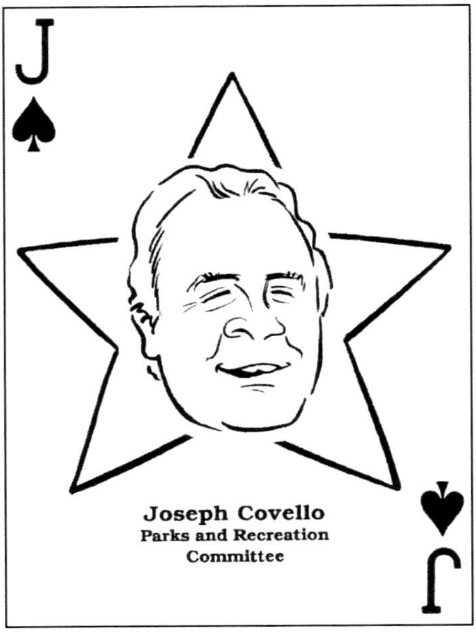

Joe Covello on a playing card, 1988. *Museum of the San Ramon Valley.*

two Catholic parishes. A joint committee composed of Pete Snyder from Dublin, Joe Covello from DSRSD and Wayne Bennett from San Ramon addressed the service issues—a more volatile group could hardly be imagined.

Finally, a memorandum of opinion was proposed in 1988 that settled out the facilities and services (such as parks, amusement and fire) and was signed by Dublin mayor Linda Jefferies and San Ramon mayor Diane Schinnerer. Byron Athan became San Ramon's first city attorney, and he viewed the service district reorganizations as an inevitable event. To him, community service districts should be viewed as "temporary custodians of local government services."

The new city council addressed myriad service and community issues and worked to unify south and north San Ramon.

Suburban San Ramon—North

Nearly a decade after the Volk/McLain development began in South San Ramon and Dublin, similar changes started in the pastoral landscape to the north. Drivers on the new I-680 freeway after 1966 saw expansive open spaces with orchards on both sides and cattle grazing on the hills. The historic village area had just a few businesses, such as San Ramon Motors, Fereira garage, Villa San Ramon and the Brass Door.

This was about to change. Businesses started to move in, scattered around the old village site for the most part. A special *Valley Pioneer* tabloid in 1967 touted the '60s as a decade of progress and said, "The unique community of San Ramon has seen widespread growth in a variety of select, 'glamour' industries." New businesses included Aeroject-General Corporation (nuclear engineering and research) and the MBA Associates (research and development in the field of rocket ordnance and survival equipment) that evidently qualified as glamorous. The Greater San Ramon Improvement Association organized in 1961 and became a voice for these businesses and the community.

Then, in 1969, rumors floated that the 1,773-acre Bishop Ranch had been sold. The weekly *Valley Pioneer* investigated the sale and shared one story that a large recreation park, Six Flags Over Texas, might locate there.

The buyer turned out to be Western Electric, a subsidiary of American Telephone and Telegraph. Western Electric needed a location to produce transmission and electronic switching equipment for use by the Bell companies. The company planned a 500,000-square foot plant with as many as two thousand employees.

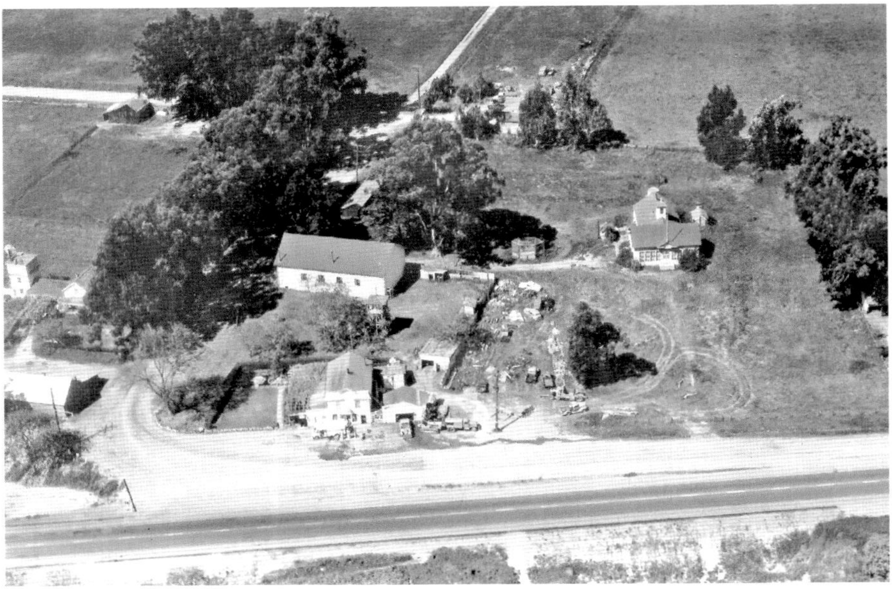

An aerial photograph of the original San Ramon Village showing a few buildings. *From left to right*: a blacksmith shop, the general store and garage are in the forefront along the old highway, and the San Ramon Hall and San Ramon Grammar School are located to the west, surrounded by ranch land, circa 1955. *Museum of the San Ramon Valley.*

Western Electric's purchase initiated San Ramon's northern growth. It hired Dan Coleman Associates to create a master plan for a new town that would include light industry, houses, stores and parks. It was presented to county planning staff, the planning commission and the board of supervisors. In record time, the new "Model City" received county planning and environmental approval. East Bay Municipal Utility District and Central Sanitary District provided essential utilities.

There was enthusiastic backing for the master plan by the San Ramon Homeowners Association, the Greater San Ramon Improvement Association and the San Ramon Valley Chamber of Commerce. Although the Western Electric project had anticipated development under one management, technological advances in its field meant it no longer needed the large plant. Western Electric began to sell the property piecemeal to several developers.

Homes were built first, beginning with Shapell Industries' Inverness Park and Dame Homes at Twin Creeks. Carl Dame's new homes at Twin Creeks seemed to always have problems, including siding quality and plumbing issues. San Ramon fire chief Bill Fereira said, in a 2007 interview, "Dame

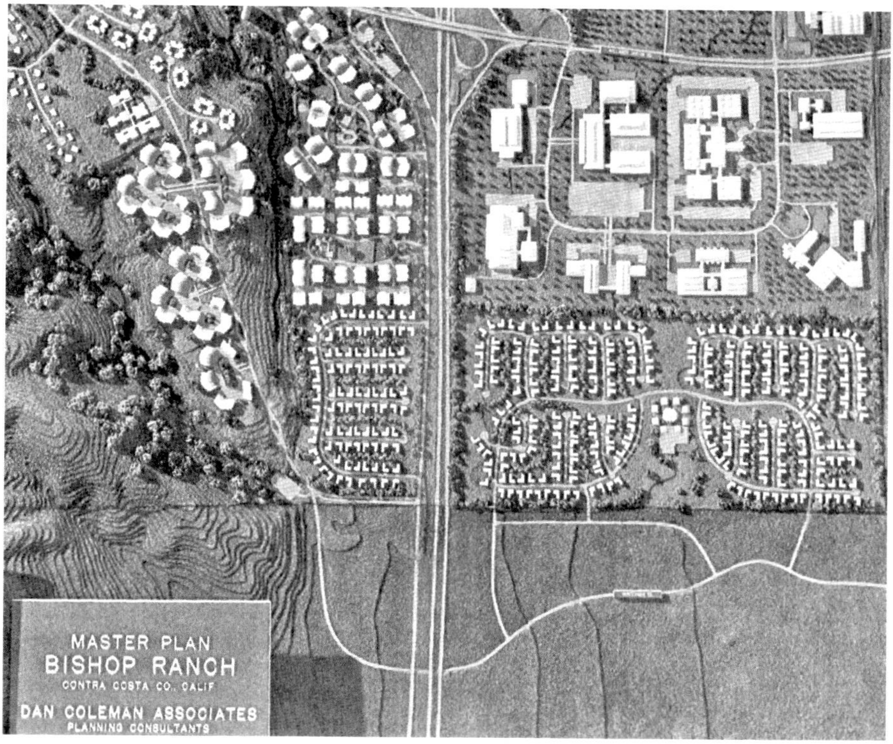

This is a copy of the southern part of the Bishop Ranch Master Plan, produced in 1971. It shows Bollinger Canyon Road at the north, the I-680 freeway to the west and Montevideo Road to the south. Shapell Home's Inverness Park is now located just south of the area zoned for controlled manufacturing; Dame's Twin Creeks developments are to the west. *Dan Coleman Jr. collection.*

pushed people around. He tried to put in fewer hydrants than the law required. He'd walk right past the girls [in the office] to come talk to me. I didn't take any flack. Dame was always in court."

In 1978, Masud and Alex Mehrans's Sunset Development Company purchased the 585 acres that were zoned for controlled manufacturing in the master plan. The company had been a homebuilder in the Livermore area. Initially, it wanted to rezone 140 acres for housing but the homeowner associations, chamber and county strongly urged the company to keep the zoning for jobs. There was widespread support for the original plan.

In the early '80s, Sunset Development needed to get income on its investment and decided to build some Class A office buildings on its property that were quickly filled. More offices were planned. Then Masud and Alex

Mehran successfully recruited both Chevron and Pacific Bell to bring their national headquarters to the newly named Bishop Ranch Business Park. The Mehrans planned 8.5 million square feet of premier office and industrial space with thirty thousand employees at build out, which would have tremendous impact on San Ramon.

As the former Bishop Ranch property in the valley developed, so did the hills on both sides.

One transformed property was the Kaplan/Wiedemann grazing land on the eastern hills. Tax pressures and assessment district costs led the owners to sell the property to Blackhawk Development Company for a homes project called Canyon Lakes. The developers planned and built a variety of housing types with 3,100 residential units in twelve different neighborhoods, an eighteen-hole golf course, a large lake, a clubhouse and recreational facilities. Grading began in 1984.

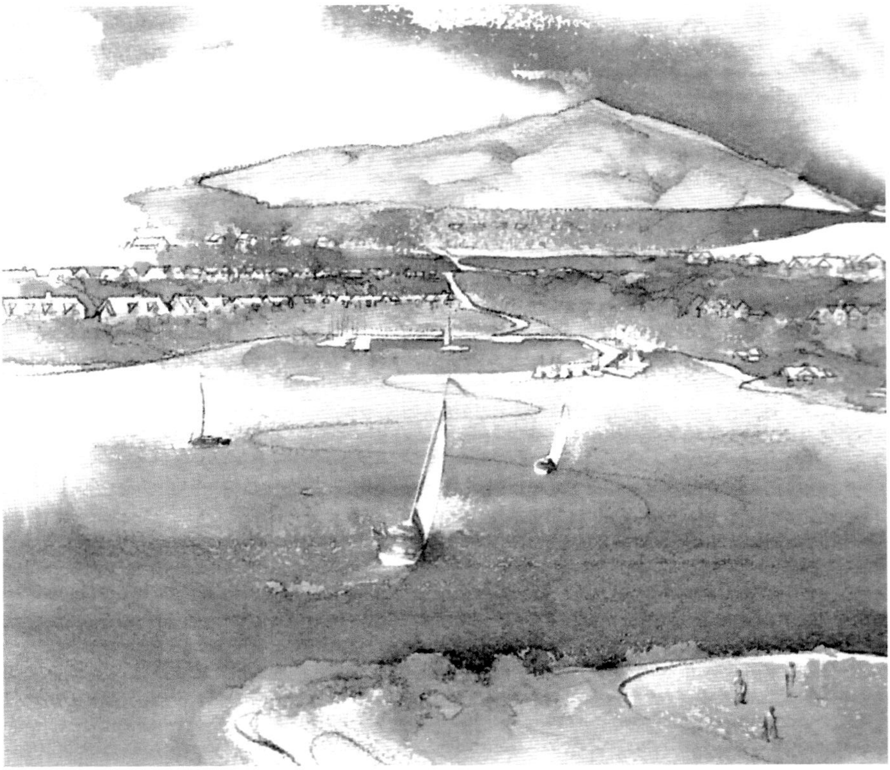

This Canyon Lakes development brochure shows homes and a lake—ranchland no more. *Museum of the San Ramon Valley.*

With homes built and jobs available, the population swelled. In 1970, San Ramon had 4,084 people; by 1975, 12,782 people; by 1980, 22,356; and by 1990, 35,303. This growth led new residents to demand more schools, parks, programs for youth and better police coverage. The Homeowners Association of Twin Creeks began as a social group for neighbors to meet one another. But soon a planning committee, energized by Pat Boom and Mary Lou Oliver, began to address county development plans and speak at the meetings.

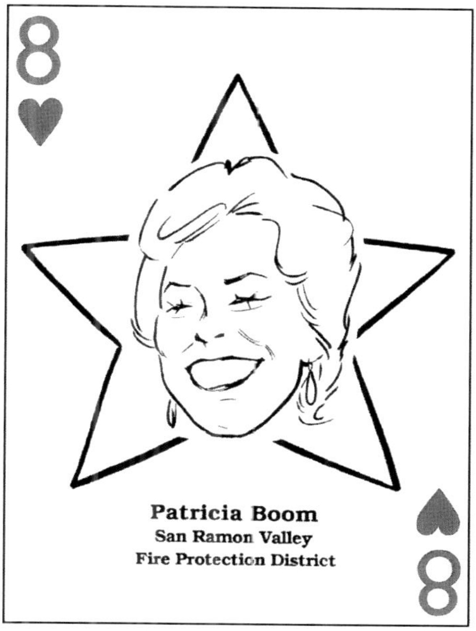

Mayor Pat Boom on a playing card, 1988. *Museum of the San Ramon Valley.*

There were three attempts to incorporate the San Ramon Valley that went to the ballot unsuccessfully in 1967, 1973 and 1976. The proposed boundary in 1967 left out Bishop Ranch and set up a two-hundred-foot corridor along the old highway to include the new homes in South San Ramon. It was ridiculed as the "cherry stem city," which helped defeat the incorporation effort at the polls.

Political debates did not go away, however. When San Ramon incorporated in 1983, Contra Costa County and Alex Mehran of Sunset Development Company kept the business park out of the city's original boundary. Five years later, Bishop Ranch Business Park was annexed to the city after lengthy negotiations. The city successfully annexed properties that surrounded the Bishop Ranch, effectively creating an unincorporated island at the city's core.

Some wags said that the Bishop Ranch had annexed San Ramon.

Bishop Ranch Business Park

When the bucolic Bishop Ranch began to develop in the 1970s, a key part of its county-adopted master plan was 585 acres zoned for controlled industry. The county board of supervisors, planners, local business and homeowner groups were keen to see the master plan's "Model City" proceed as approved.

In 1978, Masud and Alexander Mehran, a father-son team, purchased the 585 acres. Masud Mehran's Sunset Development Company had successfully built four thousand homes and offices in Livermore beginning in 1951. Alex returned to California in 1977 after school and time as a commercial banker back East, and Sunset was revitalized. Initially, the company built twenty-one homes in Alamo's Round Hill Country Club as well as some homes and office buildings in Livermore.

As Alex tells it, they began to look for a large property to purchase and settled on Bishop Ranch. It was close to a freeway, located not that far from San Francisco and had zoning approvals and certified environmental documents. At a cost of around $20 million they bought the 585 acres in October 1978. The landowner, Western Electric, helped finance the purchase. Since they had a three-year grace period with no interest, the Mehrans were eager to proceed with development and eliminate the debt on the property.

Alex relates an amusing story about going to the county office in Martinez to meet planning director Tony Dehaesus. Evidently, one of the planners he first talked to sent Dehaesus a note that said a young man wanted to meet

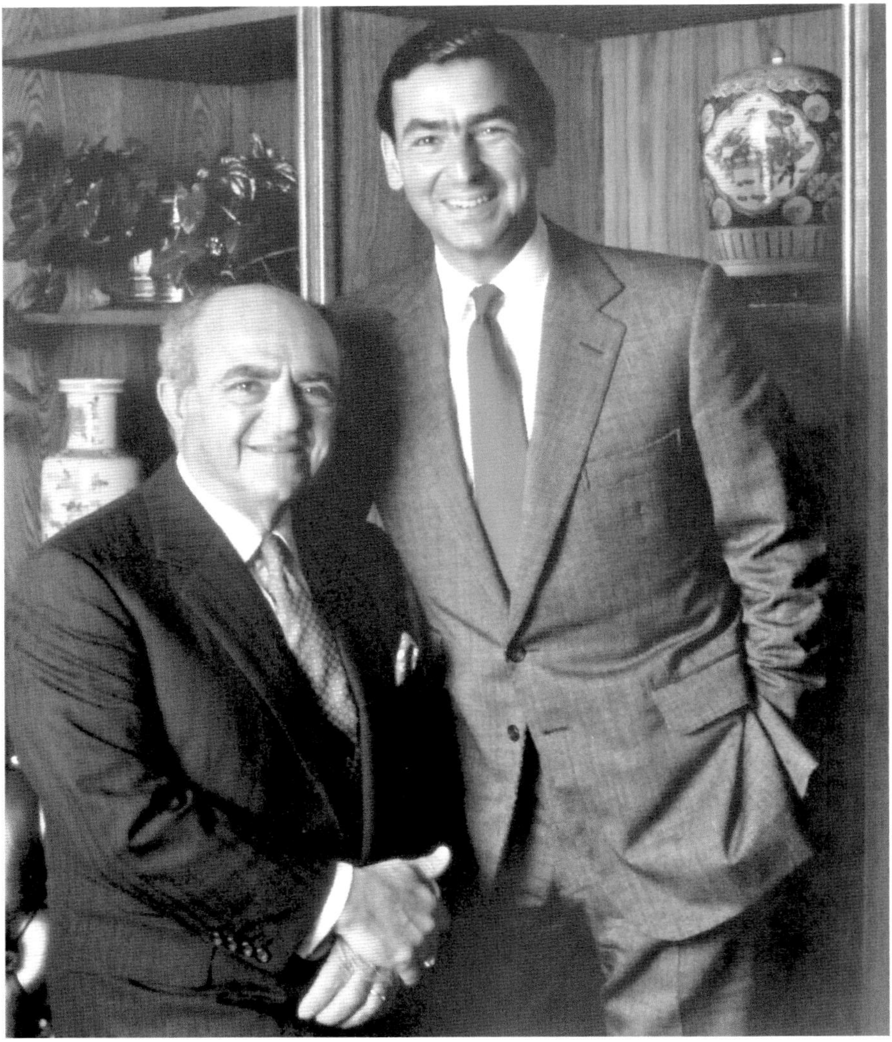

Masud and Alex Mehran of Sunset Development Company established the Bishop Ranch Business Park. *Bishop Ranch collection.*

him who "seemed to be straight and not an L.A. sharp developer." Dehaesus gave him the note later.

Because the acreage was somewhat larger than they had anticipated purchasing, the Mehans had long discussions about what should happen on the site. An economic study was done that indicated that some combination of offices, light industry and housing would work. They hired

Dan Coleman to draw a mixed-use plan with 50 industrial acres, 50 office acres, 140 residential acres and 300 undesignated acres. The local rumor mill assumed that the Mehrans planned to build homes on 100 percent of the land, since Sunset Development was known as a home developer.

When the Mehrans took this plan to the county, Dehaesus said that the community was happy with the existing zoning and sent them to meet with the San Ramon Homeowners Association. Alex said that the association had tremendous power. He and his father went to the homeowners' meeting, and he recalls "getting hammered." The association did not want housing on that acreage and was adamant about it. The duo received the same negative reception when they brought the plan to the Homeowners Association of Twin Creeks, the Danville Association and Regional Planning Commissioners. All were unanimous in saying that the area needed jobs, not more housing.

A very polite letter from the San Ramon Homeowners on August 4, 1979, stated:

> *As this parcel has been specified for Controlled Manufacturing use for many years, we are sure that you were aware of that fact before you purchased the parcel… We trust that you will direct all your efforts to the development of a full 580-acre industrial park similar to those now enjoyed by many other predominately residential communities. By doing so, you will certainly provide a lasting benefit to our community, and at the same time realize a substantial and fair profit for your company.*

It was written by Mike Wahlig, typed up by Joyce Wahlig and signed by association president Dave Stegman. With the eventual success of the business park, Wahlig later said that the Mehrans should have sent them a thank-you note.

Indeed, Sunset Development Company took a giant step away from its historic role as a homebuilder and began constructing offices. They were and are debt-averse and needed to have income from the property. First, they produced 100,000 square feet of Class A office buildings north of Norris Canyon Road. Alex said, "My dad was really nervous about doing this. He worried they wouldn't fill up." The buildings were leased out in four months. Three more office buildings were constructed and filled within twenty-four months.

Alex described himself as "being the band" and wading in to create a new business. In 1980, Beckman Instruments bought 33 acres and then

Toyota Motor Sales took 30 acres. When Standard Oil/Chevron bought 143 acres in 1982, this was the turning point for Sunset. A year later, Pacific Bell bought 100 acres. Two of the country's largest corporations placed their national headquarters in the Bishop Ranch Business Park.

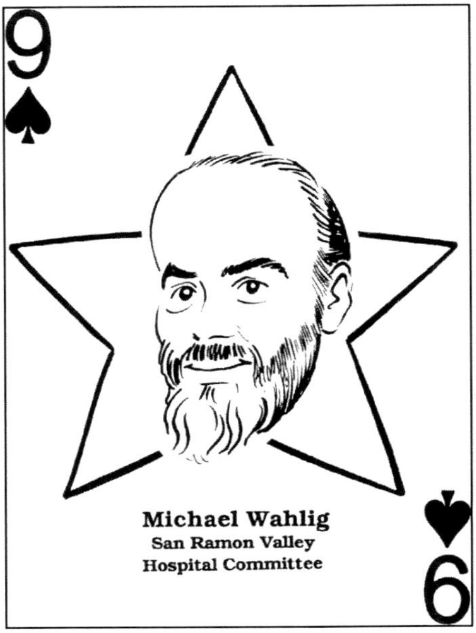

Michael Wahlig on a playing card, 1988. *Museum of the San Ramon Valley.*

It became the largest business park west of Chicago, with office space totaling 8.5 million square feet. A Marriott Hotel, transit center and the Shops at Bishop Ranch were constructed. The number of employees rose from 1,500 in 1984 to 15,000 in 1988 with an anticipated 40,000 employees at build-out. In the early years, employees moved from San Francisco and joked that they were going to "San Remote."

By 1984, Sunset had 4.5 million square feet of buildings plus roads and landscaping underway at one time. Eager to see an access from Bollinger Canyon Road into Bishop Ranch, Sunset Development contributed $2.5 million to build the interchange. It was not a decision that made them popular with other development companies. But they had $5 million worth of office space in the works and needed a direct way for employees to reach the business park.

A quality business environment was their goal. They provided unique signage, master-planned landscaping, careful selection of tenants and service to their customers. For years, Alex Mehran interviewed every single potential tenant and became proficient at deciding quickly which were best for the business park.

One of the Bishop Ranch brochures points out that its "nationally recognized 585-acre development has been pivotal to the economic growth of the San Ramon Valley and Contra Costa County." Alex Mehran's leadership transformed the county's venerable development association into the Contra Costa Council for which he served as president in the 1980s.

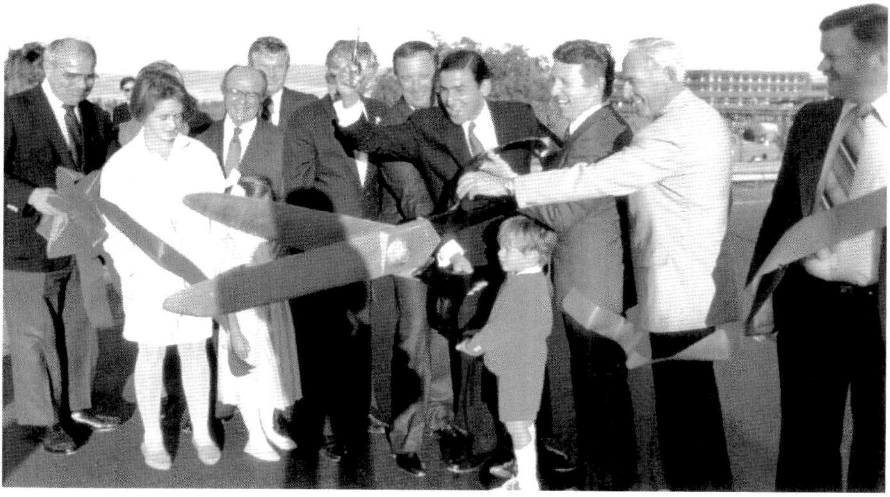

The Bollinger Canyon Interchange Dedication in 1984 at Bishop Ranch Business Park included state and local officials. *Left to right*: Tony Dehaesus, Christina Mehran, Masud Mehran, Larry Dahms, Tom Powers (behind scissors), Ed DeSilva, Alexander Mehran, Leo McCarthy, Burch Bachtold and Mike Walford. The children are Annabel Mehran and Alexander Mehran Jr. *Museum of the San Ramon Valley.*

Now called the Leadership Council of the East Bay, the organization advocates for public policies that benefit the economy and quality of life in the county and the Tri-Valley. The Contra Costa Economic Partnership is an arm of the council.

In discussions with his father about naming the business park, Alex pressed to keep the name Bishop Ranch. The family lived in Diablo Country Club when he grew up, and those local memories may have influenced this choice. Thus the historic ranch has not been forgotten.

Bishop Ranch Business Park is located in the center of San Ramon. While it was not included in the original 1983 San Ramon city boundary, the business park annexed to the city in 1988 following extensive negotiations on tax distributions and planning. Points of sales and hotel revenues come to the city. Alex Mehran has been a significant player in many San Ramon activities from donating to causes to hosting community activities, such as the Tree Lighting and Farmers Market, and discussing a prospective new city center.

Current plans for the business park will take the Bishop Ranch in a very different direction, facilitated by Alexander Mehran Jr., who joined the

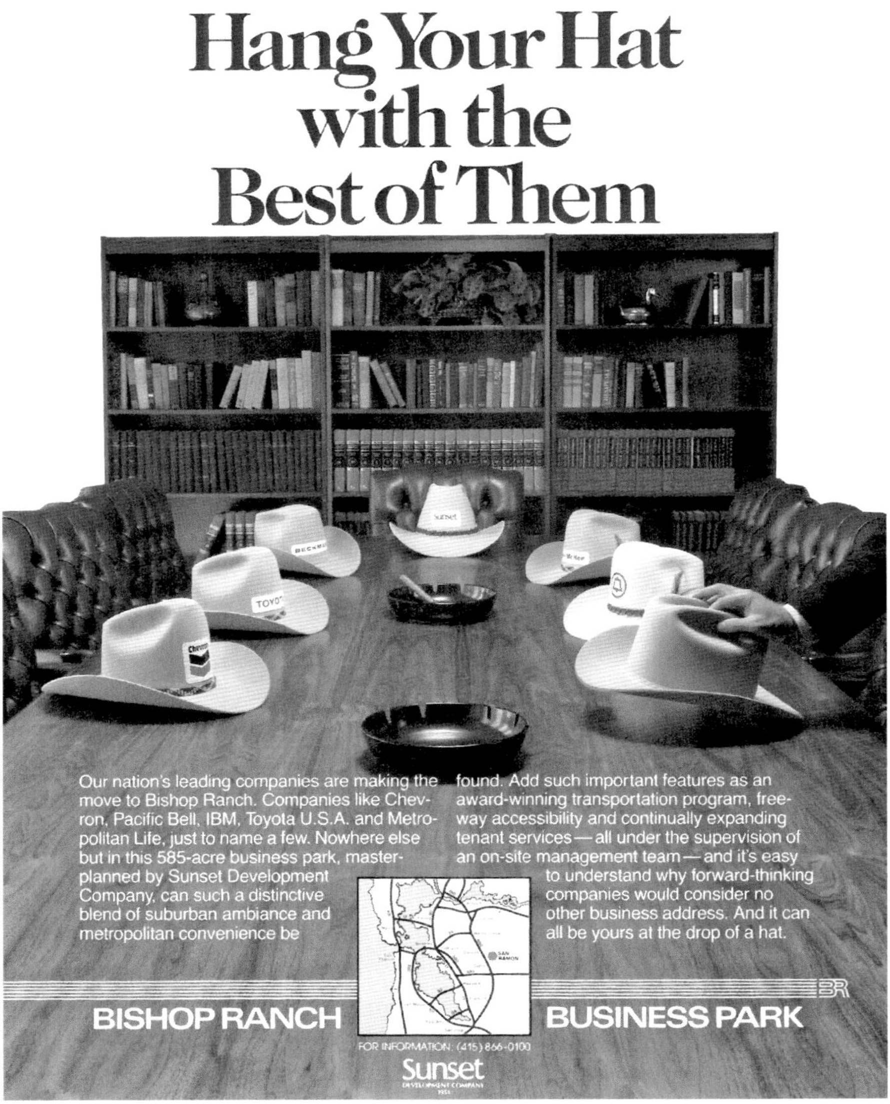

Cowboy hats provided a unique promotion for Bishop Ranch Business Park. *Bishop Ranch collection.*

company in 2011 and is now president and chief operating officer. Today, Sunset Development is advancing more green landscaping practices and organizing bicycles and car sharing. It recently received Leadership in Energy and Environmental Design (LEED) certification for twenty-eight buildings totaling 6 million square feet, which makes it one of the most ambitious LEED certifications ever undertaken by a business complex in the country.

Where formerly the park was all offices and was deserted in the evenings, today there are plans to provide what young Mehran calls "a needed and vital combination of amenities for Bishop Ranch customers, the community of San Ramon and the entire region." A new city center at Bollinger Canyon and Camino Ramon proposes 350,000 square feet of shopping, dining and entertainment around a piazza, which will create "a sense of dynamic urbanity." Antonio Belvedere of the internationally renowned Renzo Piano Building Workshop is the architect for this ambitious project that Sunset Development states is designed to be "authentic to its suburban location." A later phase will provide a hotel, more offices and five hundred residential units.

Civic facilities such as the new city hall, a renovated main library and an iconic Iron Horse Regional Trail overcrossing are currently in the works adjacent to Bishop Ranch.

Early on, Alex Mehran said that Sunset Development Company wanted to create a horizontal Rockefeller Center in the San Ramon Valley. Indeed, Bishop Ranch Business Park has become one of the nation's premier business communities with plans to expand to ten million square feet and forty thousand employees in the future. It currently includes over 550 companies, 30 industries and 37 Fortune 500 companies.

In the '70s, a dramatic shift took place as pear orchards were replaced by a "model city" with new homes and an impressive business park. Today, Bishop Ranch is evolving again from a traditional office park to what Sunset Development calls a "seven-day-a-week living, working and shopping environment." Certainly, change is in the air.

The Dougherty Valley

Today's Dougherty Valley is a rapidly growing area in San Ramon's Alamo Creek watershed. Since the late 1990s, an entirely new community has been created out of a region that was grazing land for fully two centuries.

When Mission San Jose was founded in 1797, mission territory extended into the eastern valleys of the East Bay including the San Ramon, Amador and Livermore Valleys. Over twenty thousand acres of the territory was granted to soldier Jose Maria Amador by the Mexican government in 1834. His Rancho San Ramon covered from the Dublin Hills on the west, south to I-580 and north to Crow Canyon Road. The eastern boundary included the valleys around Alamo and Tassajara Creeks. Amador's rancho grazed thousands of cattle and sheep and included a large headquarters in today's Dublin.

California's Gold Rush brought huge numbers of miners to the San Francisco Bay area. With statehood achieved in 1850, some of them came to San Ramon ready to leave mining and take up farming. They settled on Amador's Rancho San Ramon and were unwilling to acknowledge his Mexican title. Amador needed cash and was unable to evict the many squatters, so he decided to sell the land. Several Americans bought his property, including Leo Norris in 1850, Samuel Russell in 1851, Joel Harlan in 1852 and Dublin's Michael Murray and Jeremiah Fallon.

James Witt Dougherty and his family arrived in the area in early 1852, and that December, he and William Glaskin bought ten thousand acres of the rancho for $22,000. Dougherty soon became the largest landowner in

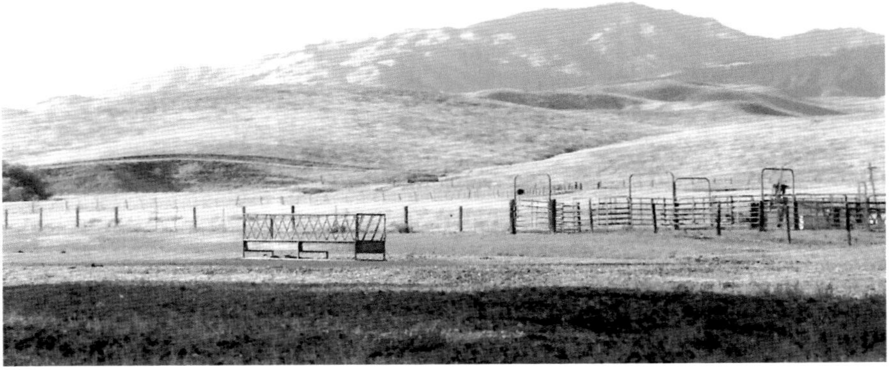

Dougherty Valley was still ranch country in 1995. This picture looks toward the north and is typical of the area before development. *Shirley Nootbaar, photographer.*

Alameda County's new Murray Township, eventually owning seventeen thousand acres in both counties. He and his wife, Elizabeth, lived in Amador's fine two-story adobe house until an earthquake in 1861 demolished it. He was elected Alameda county supervisor from the area in 1855 and was one of the largest landowners in that county.

Dougherty grazed cattle using the "DG" brand. In his later years, he worked with different breeds of horses and raised Clydesdales and Normans.

The old Amador headquarters property stood at a crossroads of two main stage roads at today's Dublin Boulevard and San Ramon Road. Several stores were erected at this well-traveled junction, and Dougherty built a hotel called Dougherty's Station, which lasted almost one hundred years. A post office, established in 1860, was likewise called Dougherty's Station, shortened to Dougherty in 1896 and discontinued in 1908.

His father migrated from Ireland, so he would have been comfortable with his many Irish neighbors. His Scotch Irish family had migrated to America in the 1700s, so he would have been comfortable with his many Irish neighbors. In the early years, the land toward the south was called Dublin while the northern area was called Dougherty.

There was another Dougherty Station that appears on the map along the Southern Pacific's San Ramon Branch Line in Alameda County, located over a mile to the east of historic Dublin. James and Elizabeth's son Charles M. Dougherty wanted to commemorate the family name in this location, but nothing was ever built there. Today, the station location is the intersection of the Iron Horse Regional Trail and Dougherty Road in Dublin.

During most of the twentieth century, the Dougherty Valley was cattle rangeland with some fields planted to grain and hay. The southern part became a military facility, Camp Parks. Several ranchers leased the land from the Dougherty family, including the Fereira, Banke, Cronin and Wiedemann families. From 1965 to 2004, Bud Nielsen's TN Cattle Company was the major tenant.

In the 1990s, the Dougherty Valley was in San Ramon's planning area, and the city expected to annex and plan development there. The valley was not far from I-680 in Contra Costa County and I-580 in Alameda County and was described by some as "infill" development close to business parks in San Ramon and Pleasanton. Development opponents predicted a congested and over-built Los Angeles in San Ramon's backyard. Five thousand acres of the Dougherty Valley had been purchased by developers Shapell Industries and Windemere Ranch Partners beginning in 1977.

When San Ramon's Council adopted a citizen-supported ordinance limiting hillside development in 1990, fewer than five thousand dwelling units could have been constructed in the valley. Asserting that they could not afford to build the area's infrastructure with so few homes, the developers turned to Contra Costa County for development approvals.

To say this was a fractious time for San Ramon would be an understatement. The city council was split over the issue, and civil meetings

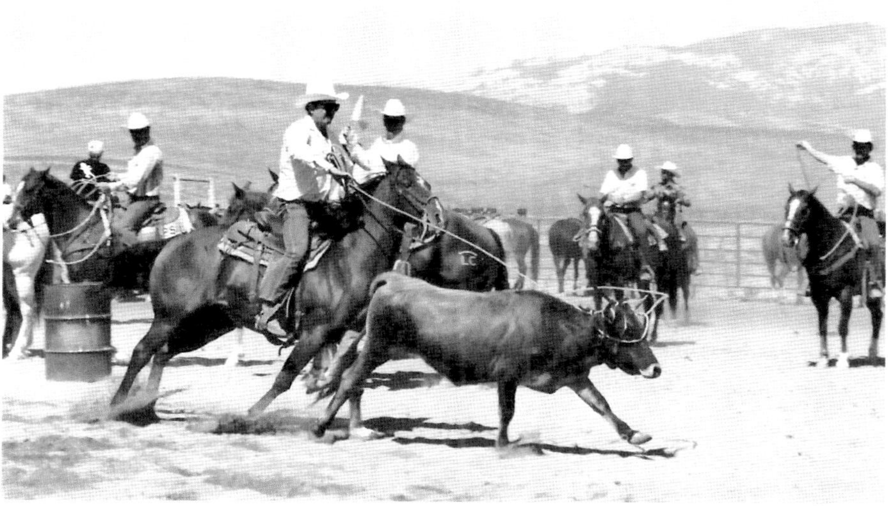

Men from Nielsen's TN Cattle Company are working cattle in this 1995 photograph. *Shirley Nootbaar, photographer.*

were a rarity. People asked why the city had incorporated when the county supervisors continued to make development decisions for San Ramon. Both San Ramon and Contra Costa County produced planning studies for the area, with nine thousand to eleven thousand residential units and different community facilities proposed.

There were water wars as well. The developers wanted to obtain East Bay Municipal Utility District (EBMUD) water for the Dougherty Valley. They tried to get legislation that would modify the water district's control over water service expansion. EBMUD sued the developers. Environmentalists on the EBMUD board who opposed extending water service to Dougherty Valley were defeated as generous campaign donations went to more amenable candidates. All this controversy was covered at length in the newspapers.

Extensive litigation on the proposed development was brought by San Ramon, four other cities, a community group and five environmental groups. Ultimately, water for most of the Dougherty Valley was obtained from the Dublin San Ramon Services District. After several contentious years, the lawsuits were settled, and a roundtable discussion with San Ramon, the county, Danville and the developers worked through the issues, leading to an agreement in 1994. A Dougherty Valley Oversight Committee was set up to monitor development compliance.

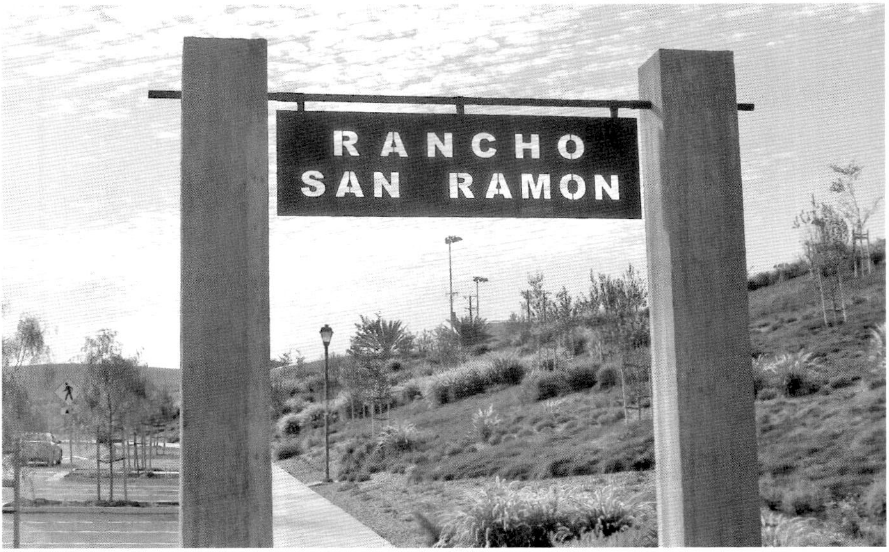

One of the Dougherty Valley community parks recalls the area's origins as Jose Maria Amador's Rancho San Ramon. *Museum of the San Ramon Valley.*

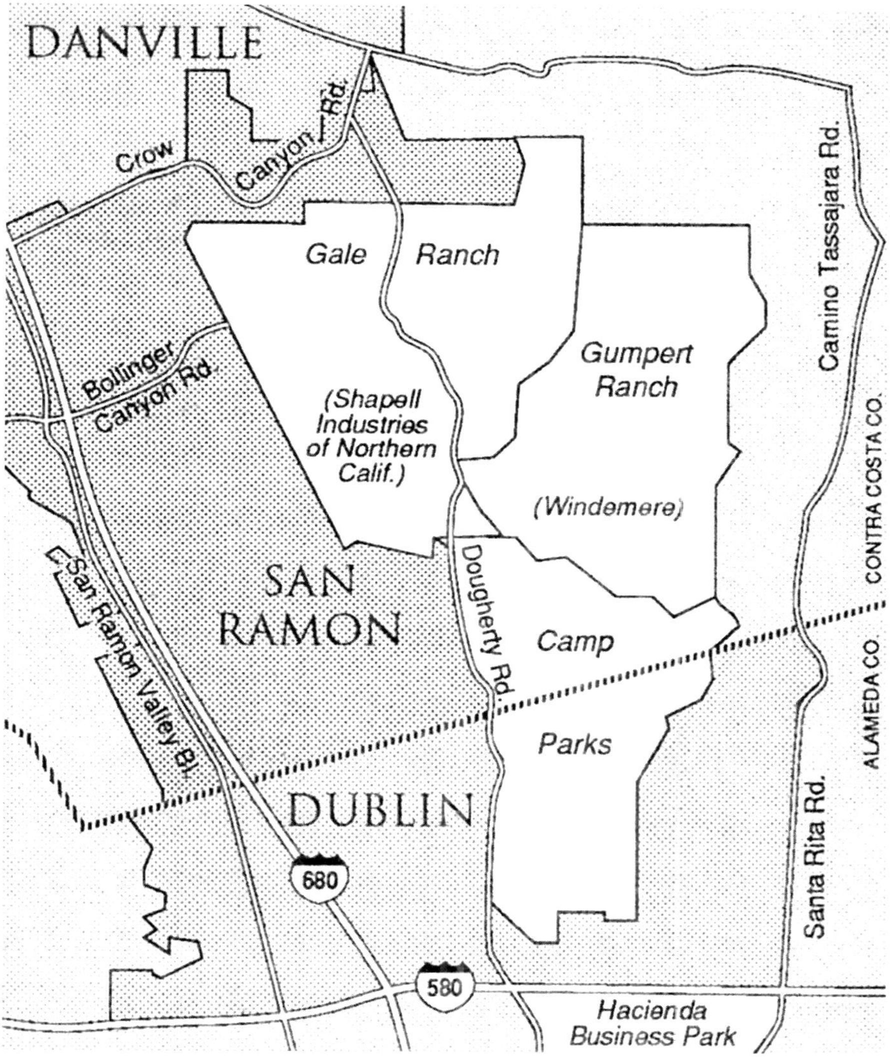

This map in 1987 shows the major sections of Dougherty Valley: Gale Ranch, Gumpert Ranch and Camp Parks total six thousand acres. *Museum of the San Ramon Valley.*

Dougherty Valley's first subdivision opened in November 1998 at the Bridges at Gale Ranch, built by Shapell Industries. These 618 acres in the region's northwest were already inside the EBMUD service area. The Bridges Golf Club opened in 1999.

With the development battles behind them, Shapell and Windemere constructed a wide variety of dwelling units, parks, landscaping, retail centers, roads and schools. They built all the community buildings, including a fire station, the Diablo Valley Community College's San Ramon campus, Dougherty Station Community Center, the Amador Rancho Center and other parks. An innovative agreement designed the Dougherty Station Library to serve both the public and the college. Several valley parks pay tribute to San Ramon's unique history, among them Limerick, San Ramon Village, Souyen, Ramona and Rancho San Ramon Community Park. The beautiful natural corridors along Alamo Creek are significant since they both protect wildlife and bring walkers to an extensive trail system. Governed by a specific plan, the valley will ultimately have eleven thousand homes.

Dougherty Valley began as mission and rancho grazing land and was ranched by the Dougherty family for 150 years. Its growth controversies mirror battles over suburban development all over the state. Now a maturing area with modern neighborhoods and distinctive community facilities, in many ways the valley's history is a microcosm of California's history.

San Ramon Embraces Cityhood

The city of San Ramon celebrated its thirtieth anniversary on July 1, 2013. While residents might assume the city has always been in place, there are many people still around who worked on San Ramon's successful incorporation campaign in 1983.

The community began in 1852, when the first post office was established in Samuel Russell's house. During the nineteenth and most of the twentieth centuries, San Ramon remained a tiny village at the crossroads of the old highway, the road to Crow Canyon and San Ramon Creek. It was surrounded by vast orchards and ranches.

After World War II, California's population exploded, and when the freeway came to Danville in 1964 and to San Ramon in 1966, the whole San Ramon Valley began to change. San Ramon had around three hundred people in 1960 and over twenty thousand by 1980.

Homeowners organized and began to speak on behalf of the new residents. The San Ramon Homeowners Association in the south and the Homeowners Association of Twin Creeks in the north commented on proposed county developments, as did the San Ramon Valley Chamber of Commerce's planning committee. The Greater San Ramon Improvement Association represented several of the new businesses in the '60s. Some of these activists won elected office on boards governing schools, fire protection and the Dublin San Ramon Services District.

Efforts to create a city for the entire San Ramon Valley began in the '60s. There were three unsuccessful incorporation votes that included

San Ramon in 1967, 1973 and 1976, all supported by San Ramon voters. Advocates wanted improved police services, parks, planning and roads. Opponents worried about the possibility of higher taxes and were usually satisfied with county government. Often, developers contributed to the opposition campaigns.

Bishop Ranch was always an issue when these new-city boundaries were proposed. Western Electric bought the ranch in 1969 and opposed being included inside any new city. It preferred developing as part of the county, whose leaders and staff they knew. The first cityhood attempt, in 1967, had a boundary that included all of Alamo and Danville, with a narrow two-hundred-foot corridor of land on the west side (skirting the ranch) that picked up South San Ramon. This boundary was successfully derided by incorporation opponents as a "cherry stem city."

By 1980, groups in Dublin, Danville and San Ramon organized and wanted to incorporate their own communities. A vote took place in 1979 that would have created an unusual San Ramon/Dublin city that crossed the Contra Costa–Alameda County line. San Ramon voted against it by a large margin. Then, in December 1981, Dublin voters incorporated as a city, and in June 1982, Danville voters did the same.

San Ramon volunteers organized the San Ramon Incorporation Study Committee in 1979 as a nonprofit corporation. San Ramon had some special challenges because its traditional downtown was in the north, and the first suburban development was in the south. Committee president Joe Covello said that he and Mary Lou Oliver eventually agreed to address the "two San Ramons" later and win incorporation first.

Later, Covello said it all started because "we were literally the tail on the dog [for the county]…We were paying more taxes than anyone and weren't getting a thing for it. There was like one policeman responsible for a large area and we hardly ever saw him."

San Ramon leaders met with county supervisor Robert Schroder and convinced him that their community deserved the chance to vote on incorporation. By 1980, a City of San Ramon would be larger than many other cities in the county. Pro-city campaign volunteers came from homeowners, service clubs, seniors, sport groups and some business owners.

The study committee overcame several barriers before the cityhood issue got to the ballot. The original fourteen founders (twelve families) of the study committee contributed $500 each to pay $6,000 to local government consultant William R. Zion for an "official" feasibility study to validate the study committee's version. Zion wrote, "My analysis finds that fiscally and operationally, incorporation is highly feasible. Few communities I have studied have as sound a tax base or city needs and costs as manageable as in San Ramon."

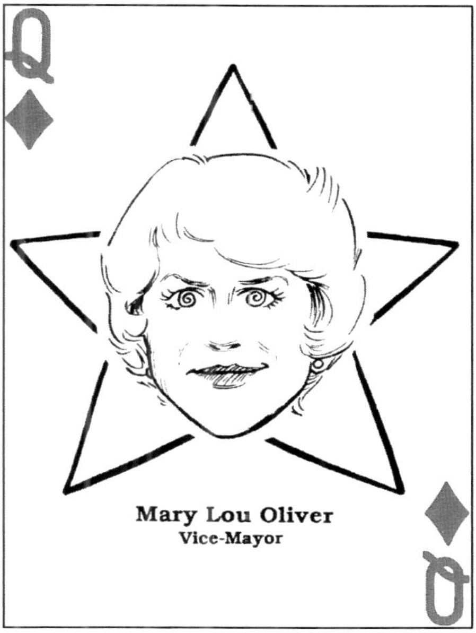

Mayor Mary Lou Oliver on a playing card, 1988. *Museum of the San Ramon Valley.*

One major hurdle was the Local Agency Formation Commission (LAFCO) and its executive officer Dewey Mansfield. LAFCO had been set up to promote orderly growth for special districts and cities. Mansfield had opposed a separate incorporation vote for Danville in 1982, reluctantly supporting it when his commission made it clear it would allow such a vote. He wanted the whole San Ramon Valley to incorporate, even though the earlier valley-wide votes had failed. He then proposed that, if San Ramon wanted to incorporate, it could annex to Danville.

At the July 10, 1982 LAFCO meeting, Mansfield recommended against holding a San Ramon–only election. The San Ramon activists spoke eloquently in favor of a San Ramon incorporation vote. Speakers included Dublin San Ramon Services District board members Diane Schinnerer, Joe Covello and Richard Fahey; former San Ramon Valley School Board member Mike Wahlig; fire district director Pat Boom; homeowner leaders Mary Lou Oliver and Thomas Bret; and the Incorporation Study Committee's first president, Rick Harmon. The commission overruled Mansfield's recommendation. The *Times* reported: "Soon after the decision cityhood backers erupted into jubilant cheers."

The reporter also noted signs of sharp politicking around the LAFCO meeting that focused on San Ramon's boundary. The W.R. Grace Development, which built the Crow Canyon Commons, tried to be omitted (with Mansfield's support) but was kept inside.

The 585-acre Bishop Ranch Business Park was excluded from the boundary. Owners Alex and Masud Mehran were at a crucial point in their planning and did not want to risk a new and unknown city council potentially altering their development plans. Supervisor Schroder (who was also chairman of LAFCO) and the other county supervisors supported the exclusion. At the time, more than fifteen thousand local jobs were expected to locate at Bishop Ranch.

Bishop Ranch's omission from the proposed city boundary was brought up in every single debate and news article. Some predicted the issue would defeat incorporation, and early polls agreed.

But a vigorous grass-roots campaign touted autonomy and the "4 Ps" for San Ramon: better public works, improved parks, increased public safety and responsive planning. "Let's Spend San Ramon Money on Improving San Ramon!" announced one brochure. Eighteen candidates tossed hats

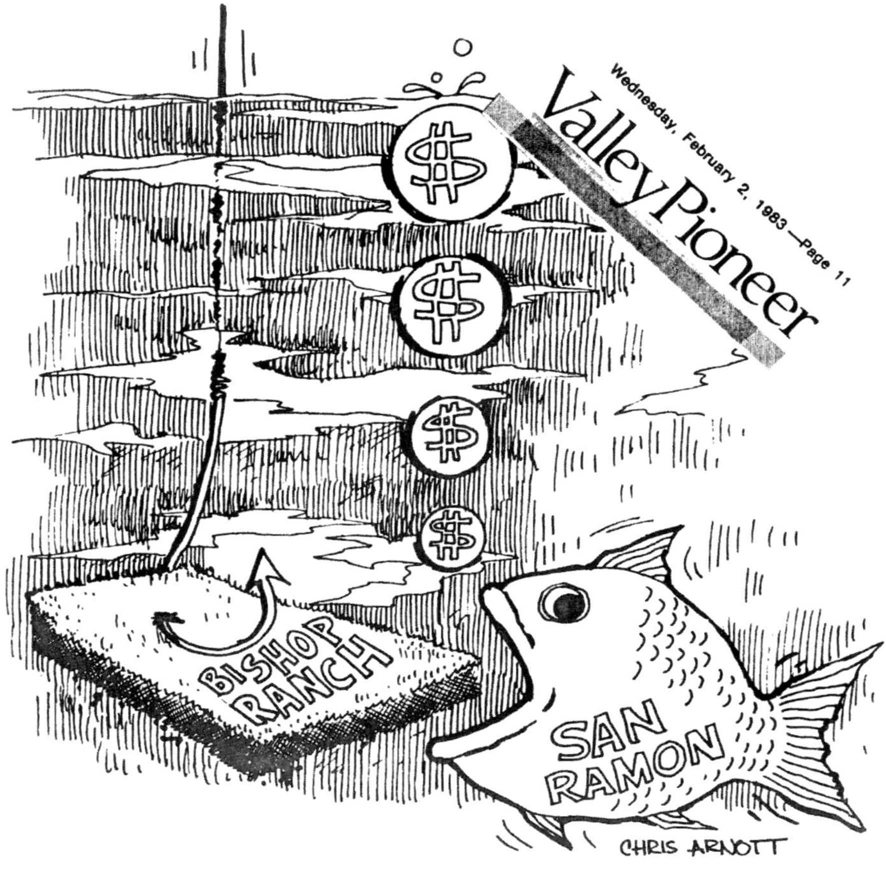

Chris Arnott drew this cartoon showing San Ramon eating Bishop Ranch in the *Valley Pioneer* on February 2, 1983. *Museum of the San Ramon Valley.*

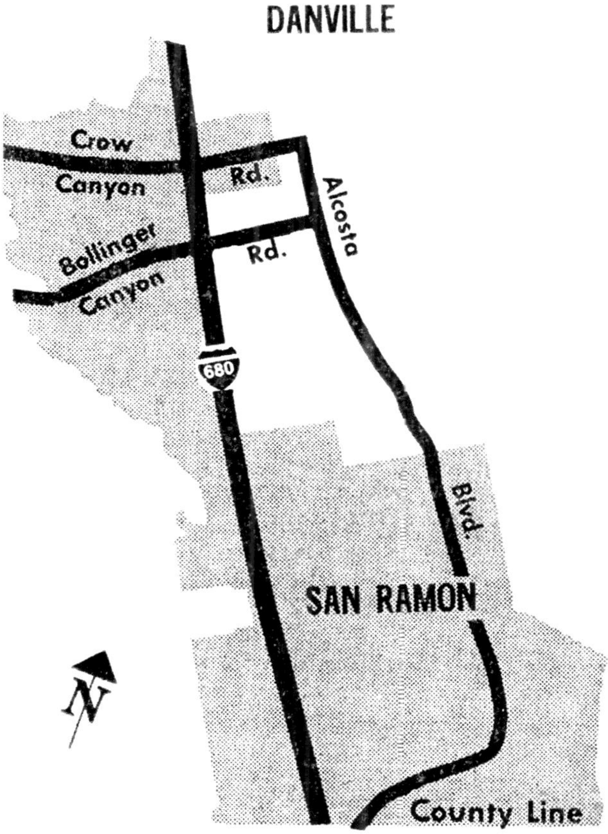

This map shows the San Ramon city boundaries that voters considered in the incorporation election on March 8, 1983, with Bishop Ranch Business Park omitted. *Museum of the San Ramon Valley.*

into the ring, with two opposed to the whole idea and one who wanted to annex to Danville. Many pledged that a new city would provide a unique identity for San Ramon.

On election day, March 8, 1983, a whopping 75 percent of the voters supported incorporation by a 3,825 to 1,254 vote. They chose a new city council: Diane Schinnerer (3,249), Rick Harmon (2,504), Mary Lou Oliver (2,459), Wayne Bennett (2,014) and Jerry Ajlouny (1,828). With new cities of Danville and Dublin to the north and south, voters clearly agreed it was the time for San Ramon's own independence.

The City's First Decades

At last, their own city. How sweet it was. Leading the way was San Ramon's first city council: Diane Schinnerer, Rick Harmon, Mary Lou Oliver, Wayne Bennett and Jerry Ajlouny.

On July 1, 1983, San Ramon formally took its place as the seventeenth city in Contra Costa County, with a population of 22,356 people. Diane Schinnerer was elected mayor by the council. The council's first formal meeting was held at California High School, followed by a three-day celebration. The new council members talked to everyone, enlisted volunteer help and happily released balloons during the park events.

Mayor Schinnerer said, "We finally got what we wanted. Now we have a lot of work to do, and I expect all of you to come forward and help." Retired county administrator George Gaekle was brought on board to help with the city's organization as he had with both Dublin and Danville. He worked with the council to set up initial ordinances, trained a city clerk, provided sage advice and searched for the first city manager. The council chose James Robinson as city manager, who addressed the new city's challenges and responded to the council's many ideas and demands.

In the first months of incorporation, the council and new manager began to address the "4 Ps": planning, police, public works and parks. The city annexed properties along Alcosta Boulevard. After lengthy negotiations between the county, the city and the Mehrans, Bishop Ranch Business Park annexed to the city in 1988. A tax agreement with the county was signed and is still in place three decades later.

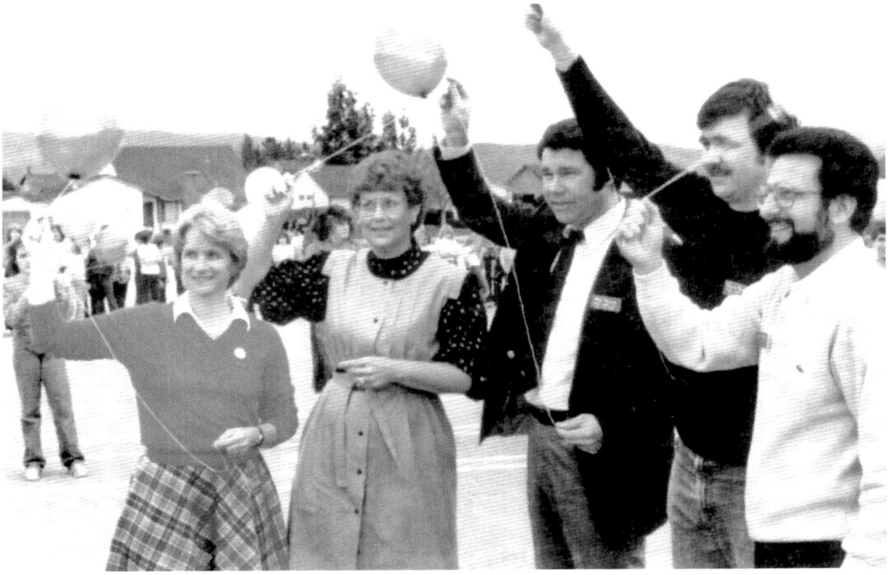

The new San Ramon Council celebrates with balloons at the park. *Left to right*: Mary Lou Oliver, Diane Schinnerer, Rick Harmon, Wayne Bennett and Jerry Ajlouny. *Museum of the San Ramon Valley.*

Soon after incorporation, several new community groups brought vital energy and ideas to the city. These included the San Ramon Chamber of Commerce, San Ramon Rotary, San Ramon Soroptimists, San Ramon Library Foundation, San Ramon American Association of University Women and a San Ramon Homeowners Council. In its 1986 report, the chamber said it had 550 members after only two years in existence.

A new logo for the city was chosen from 150 entries. It displayed a sunrise, a crow, a tree and San Ramon's incorporation date. Two San Ramon residents, Karen Winefer and Chad Hamill, shared a $100 award for designing it.

In the first decade, the city stretched its muscles and promptly addressed several planning projects. The council adopted a new sphere of influence in 1984 and its first General Plan and downtown specific plan in 1986. The Westside Specific Plan followed in 1989. Some of these specific plans were underwritten by landowners. Citizen support for open space preservation led the city council to adopt a restrictive hillside preservation ordinance in 1990, and voters rejected an expanded growth boundary in 2010. General Plans were adopted in 1986, 1995, 2002, 2011 and 2015.

The original San Ramon logo was designed by Karen Winefer and Chad Hammill. *Museum of the San Ramon Valley.*

Early on, the city planned and built Central Park at Alcosta Boulevard and Bollinger Canyon Road. The park's handsome new San Ramon Community Center opened in 1989 and made a statement that the city had arrived. It showed San Ramon's commitment to outstanding civic building design. The council, staff and citizens wanted to be much more than "San Remote."

The city's first city clerk, Judy McFarlane, pointed out that the council chose to build a community center, a library and a senior center and forgo building a city hall. For a few months, the new council discussed placing city offices in the classic 1877 Glass house to help recognize San Ramon's history. City administrative services and an unpretentious council chamber have been at 2226 Camino Ramon for thirty years. San Ramon became a charter city in 1997 and was recognized as a Tree City USA in 2001.

The council promoted childcare at businesses and at schools, added bus service from the County Connection and provided teen programs. During the early '80s, a nineteen-member Committee on Hospital Proposals representing the entire San Ramon Valley was led by Mike Wahlig and helped bring the San Ramon Regional Medical Center to the city. The city served seniors at the original White House center, dedicated as a new senior facility in 1992. It now provides the Alcosta Senior and Community Center in that location.

The council regularly supported partnerships to achieve its goals. Byron Athan was important in all these collaborative conversations. Experienced in government services, he was the city's first attorney, was elected to the council, was mayor and served as an interim city manager twice.

Changes in the business landscape occurred all over the city. In 1989, after many years with a jazzy neon sign in place, the (in)famous topless bar the Wicked Eye on San Ramon Valley Boulevard closed, to be replaced with a commercial building. It was the last topless bar in the East Bay and had the only public pool table in town. The March 8, 1989 *San Ramon Valley Times* wrote, "Wicked Eye dancers have danced their last dance in San Ramon."

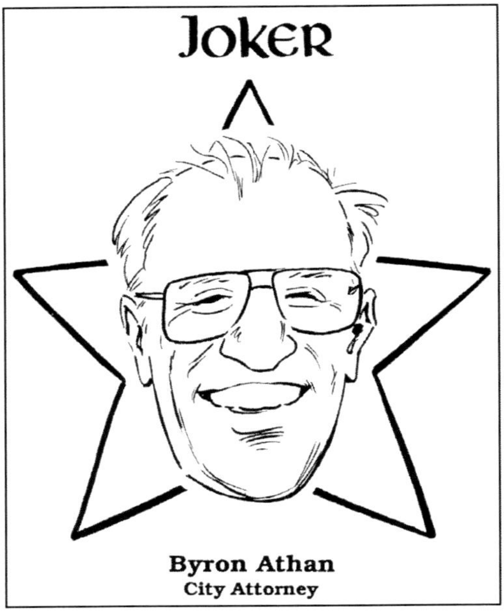

Mayor Byron Athan on a playing card, 1988. *Museum of the San Ramon Valley.*

Mudd's Restaurant opened in 1980, pioneering the California cuisine movement and focusing on tasty, fresh food. Council members met often at Mudd's, making the site a power center for the new city. In 2008, the city purchased the buildings and the adjacent Crow Canyon Gardens. In 1989, the 375-room Marriott Hotel at Bishop Ranch opened, the first of several in the city. Four San Ramon retail centers over 125,000 square feet in size serve patrons today.

Public safety has improved dramatically for San Ramon. While initially the city contracted for police services and dispatch with the county, on July 1, 2007, it created an independent San Ramon Police Department and chose Scott Holder as the first police chief. Today, six police beats cover the city. In 2015, a national rating group, Neighborhood Scout, announced that San Ramon is one of the safest cities of its size in the nation.

Herb Moniz was parks director before becoming San Ramon's city manager in 1988. With Moniz's support, parks became a special San Ramon focus. For years, residents had advocated for public recreation facilities through the Dublin San Ramon Services District in South San Ramon and County Service Area R-7 in Danville and north San Ramon. He and Jeff Eorio (director of parks and community services for twenty years) developed a parks master plan with generous goals of twelve and a half acres per thousand residents.

Parks on school sites became a signature city program with quality parks and gymnasiums distributed throughout the community. Moniz said, "The program worked really, really well because everyone wanted it. The school, the city council and community saw the benefit of it."

The East Bay Regional Park District provides several regional parks around San Ramon, including Las Trampas Wilderness and Bishop Ranch Open Space on the west and Sycamore Valley Open Space to the north.

Extensive trails allow users to take advantage of the city's moderate weather. The Iron Horse Regional Trail cuts a swath north to south through the city for 4.24 miles, the Calaveras Ridge Trail meanders over the western hills and a Tassajara Ridge Trail extends along the east side through San Ramon's Hidden Hills Open Space. Trails along both branches of Alamo Creek and a major east–west Cross Valley Trail all serve residents.

Public art required by the city in new developments enriches retail spaces throughout the city. Recently, two art pieces were installed at Athan Downs and the Sports Park. The Dougherty Valley Performing Arts Center is important to the city's theater scene and has a generous six-hundred-seat capacity. Recognizing that the wind is a regular feature of the city, the Art and Wind Festival in Central Park is a highlight of each year and draws forty thousand plus people with food and merchandise booths, fabulous kite flying and diverse entertainment.

Many of the parks have historic themes or names with wayside panels to help residents understand the city's earlier period. Council member Pat Boom talked with Ruth Quayle Boone about San Ramon's lengthy agricultural past, and Mrs. Boone decided to donate the sixteen-acre Boone Ranch's headquarters to the city. It is now the Forest Home Farms Historic Park and honors both Ruth and her husband, Travis Boone. The Eliza and David Glass house was saved, restored and moved to Forest Home Farms. Two parks are named for advocates Byron Athan and Dick Fahey, who fought for parks in San Ramon well before the city incorporated.

A new San Ramon library was supported by the Library Foundation Board, which was an impressive public-private partnership. Volunteers raised funds and purchased a remarkable initial collection of thirty thousand books. The library opened in 1989 to great fanfare and was the first library built in the county after

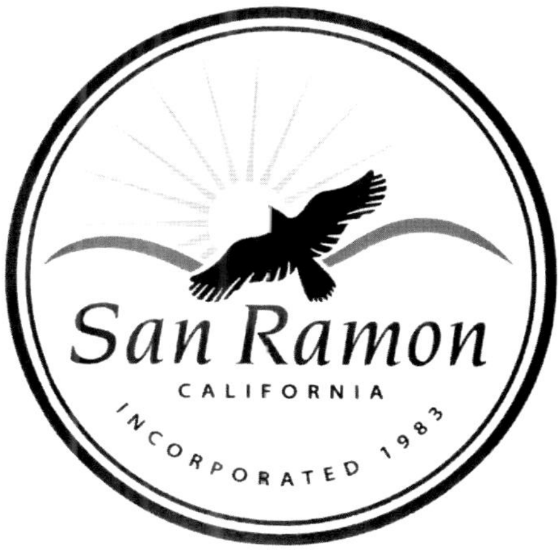

The modern San Ramon city seal. *San Ramon City Collection.*

Proposition 13 decreased property taxes. The Dougherty Station Library opened in 2005.

Voters chose to have an independently elected mayor in 2003 instead of using the council rotation system. Since that time, H. Abram Wilson and Bill Clarkson have served as mayors. Greg Rogers became city manager in 2011.

Thirty years later, the thriving city has grown from 22,356 to 78,820 people and is now the fourth largest city in Contra Costa County. It has expanded from 7.1 square miles in 1983 to 18.66 square miles in 2015. In partnership with Sunset Development, a new city center is in the works, providing upscale retail, hotel and restaurant spaces around a piazza at Bishop Ranch. Civic projects include a new city hall, a renovated main library and an Iron Horse Regional Trail overcrossing at Bollinger Canyon Road.

Former mayor Byron Athan said, "No doubt about it—city government is the first line of government. It's where citizens have the most influence." Addressing his vision for the city, in 2003, Mayor H. Abram Wilson said, "The future is going to be exciting and dynamic…We all have the same goal to make San Ramon the envy of all cities in the United States." As the city's website modestly notes, San Ramon is one of the San Francisco Bay Area's premier communities.

Where IS San Ramon?

Just where is San Ramon? For decades, a unique downtown, a recognized central gathering place and a sense of community identity have been missing.

By the time San Ramon incorporated in 1983, its historic downtown village was gone. The San Ramon grammar school, general store, shoe shop, church and community hall were no more. Only the mature eucalyptus trees remained along Old Crow Canyon Road, now renamed Deerwood Road.

San Ramon grew from both ends, with the first suburban homes built at the south and the Bishop Ranch Master Plan of 1971 adopted at the north. To add to the mix, Dougherty Valley developed in the late '90s, bringing a surge of new residents from the city's east who needed connections with the community.

During the incorporation campaign, city council candidates promised to address a unique identity for San Ramon. Gerald Rowley, who came in sixth, said, "Cityhood will give us a fantastic identity that has been missing." Rick Harmon stated that it is important for San Ramon's identity that it look distinctive. Diane Schinnerer wanted to beautify the town and give it an identity.

Valley Pioneer columnist Clay Kallam predicted in 1983, "San Ramon could well be the Walnut Creek for the 1990's, except it will lack a cohesive downtown area."

After cityhood in 1983, the council and others repeatedly called for a distinctive downtown that they could point to as the center of the city.

Activist Joe Covello said, "The north and south parts of town didn't really want to join [together,] and we had this Bishop Ranch blob in the middle." He described San Ramon as "schizophrenia city."

What were the city's options? One was the original San Ramon historic village site. What about building a new downtown and community buildings northwest of Crow Canyon Road and San Ramon Valley Boulevard? The new San Ramon Chamber of Commerce appointed a committee to help create this downtown. On the committee were city council members, planning commissioners, chamber and homeowner representatives and local business and property owners.

In 1986, San Ramon's first General Plan included a downtown specific plan for that area that was adopted by the council. A major purpose was to create a centralized focal area with a "downtown feeling." While they wanted a retail focus, one secondary goal was to "create a positive sense of place within the Downtown that reinforces San Ramon as a unique city."

For years, city-landowner discussions about modernizing this proposed "downtown" area waxed and waned. A redevelopment area proposal was resisted by landowners. The many businesses in the area covered by the downtown-specific plan provided substantial tax support for the city. Businesses varied from the Outpost, which had opened in 1978 as a "saloon styled card club," to a farmers' market, auto shops, restaurants and home supply stores. There were plenty of spoons stirring the proposed downtown soup.

A second option was the Central Park area at Alcosta Boulevard and Bollinger Canyon Road. It was centrally located and adjacent to vacant property owned by Bishop Ranch Business Park. By 1989, the San Ramon Community Center, Central Park and the main library had opened, providing important civic uses.

A third option then appeared. After a decade of unsuccessful downtown specific plan implementation, in 1996, San Ramon planning director Phil Wong, city manager Herb Moniz and Sunset Development

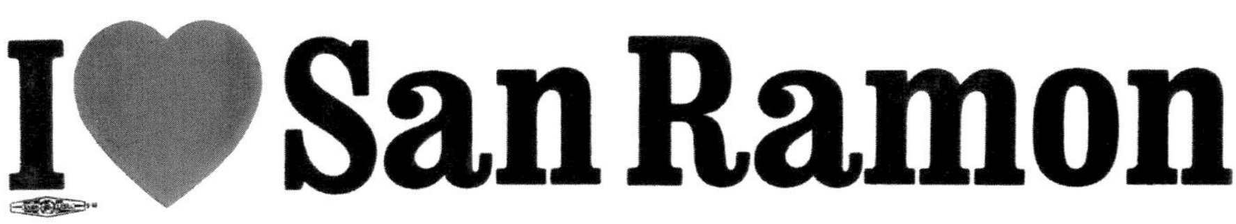

This "I Love SR banner" was sold to raise funds for the 1983 incorporation campaign with a donation of $5.00 for two or $3.00 each. *Museum of the San Ramon Valley.*

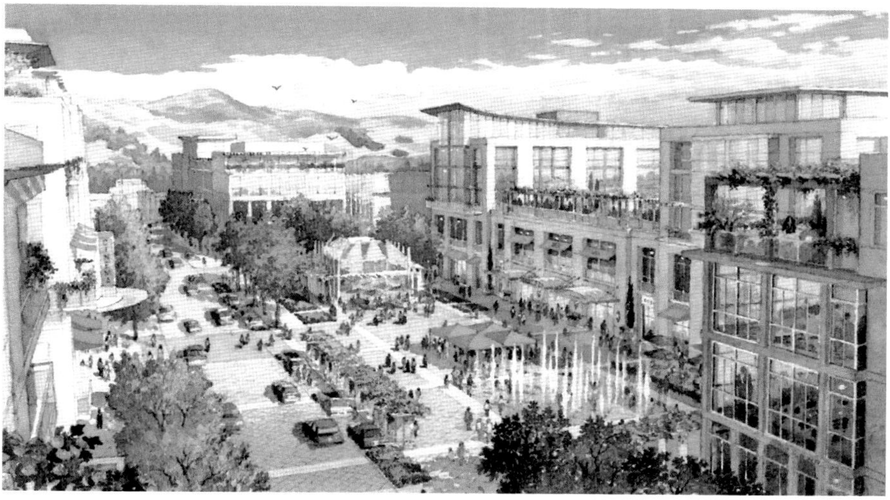

A 2007 drawing of the city center piazza at Bishop Ranch Business Park shows what an enticing area it could be. *Bishop Ranch Business Park collection.*

Company's Alex Mehran discussed a possible new collaboration focused on Bollinger Canyon Road and Camino Ramon. Bishop Ranch Business Park was doing well, drawing extraordinary national attention and putting San Ramon on the map. Mehran was game to propose ideas for a city center, and of course, he liked his own way. Sometimes these conversations went smoothly, sometimes not.

Lively public discussions on the topic ensued. Weighing in were Mehran, city manager Moniz, the San Ramon mayors, city council members, planners and an opinionated public. All the debates were covered with great gusto by the press. In 1997, Mehran dramatically called an end to Sunset Development's involvement in a city center at yet one more acrimonious council meeting.

A decade later, another city center plan proposed in 2007 would have created a new city hall and main library located south of Bollinger Canyon Road near the Iron Horse Trail and built upscale retail inside Bishop Ranch. The next year, the national economic crisis put these plans on hold.

In the meantime, the city had many opportunities to shape its identity, creating distinctive signage and landscaped roads. It built well-loved parks, libraries and community centers and sponsored myriad recreation programs. By 2015, there were fifty-six parks, two Olympic pool complexes, two theaters, two libraries, the Glass house museum, Forest Home Farms

Historic Park and two community gardens. Trails linked neighborhoods throughout the city.

San Ramon's 2015 population was 78,820, which reflected the rapid expansion of Dougherty Valley in the previous decade. This growth provides the current identity challenge. The Dougherty Valley population is younger than other parts of the city, has a population per household of 3.32 compared to 2.85 elsewhere and includes more multigenerational families. Complicating efforts to create a citywide community identity is the region's diverse racial make up, with many more Southeast and Indian Asians moving into the valley than live in the older parts of the city.

In 2003, Mayor H. Abrams Wilson asserted, "Some are saying there is Dougherty Valley and there is San Ramon Valley…There is really only San Ramon, period…We have different areas in the community now, and it's like we are one hand. This will be another one of the fingers on the same hand."

But still, where—and what—is San Ramon?

Today, the city and Sunset Development are creating a new city center, a convergence of resident and employee activities at Bollinger Canyon Road, Camino Ramon and Central Park. Antonio Belvedere of the celebrated Renzo Piano Building Workshop is designing the city center facilities at Bishop Ranch. Sunset Development Company president Alexander Mehran Jr. recently said, "We're trying to create a downtown…and a community connection. Our goal is to build a beautifully designed, enduring neighborhood for the entire region."

In 2016, the long-awaited city hall—designed by Ted Korth, Jim Sunseri and Greg Hagey—will be dedicated. A renovated main library

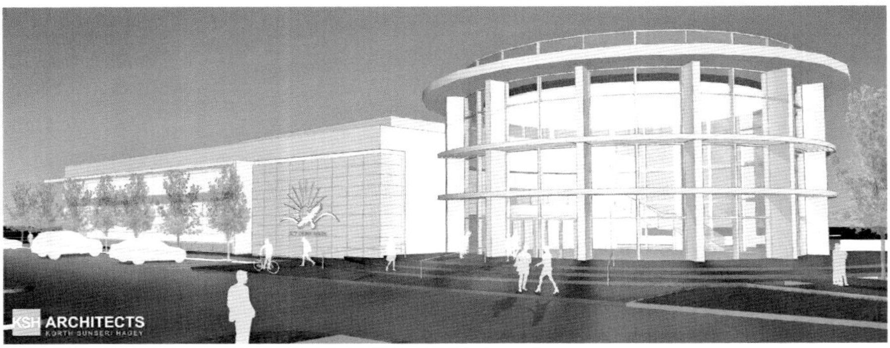

A drawing of the new San Ramon City Hall, built by Korth Sunseri Hagey. It opens to the public in 2016. *San Ramon City collection.*

with a new entry facing city hall will open in 2017, and a signature Iron Horse Trail bridge will cross over Bollinger Canyon Road. In Bishop Ranch, the city center will feature a large piazza, surrounded by pavilions with retail spaces and an upscale movie theater. Later phases will include residential units, a hotel, additional retail, more plazas and offices. These new structures are planned to draw in and engage both the community and business park employees.

With stunning new buildings and a desire to express San Ramon's unique identity, these latest plans may well provide the longed-for sense of place which city leaders have pursued for fully three decades.

Appendices

San Ramon Fire Protection District 1963–80

(Some Commissioners served until the district merged with the San Ramon Valley Fire Protection District)

1963 Commissioners

Larry Davidson
Armand Borel
Mickey Schlesinger
Howard Wiedemann
A.C. "Johnny" Johnson

San Ramon Incorporation Study Committee

Incorporated as a nonprofit in 1979, this committee successfully campaigned to create the City of San Ramon on March 8, 1963.

Mary Lou Oliver
Pat Boom
Judy Macfarlane
Rick Harmon (original president)
Mike and Joyce Wahlig
Debbie and Jim Hughes
Gerry O'Brien
Don Jones
Nancy Eschen
Ora Hed
Bill Box
Joe Covello (president during the final months of the campaign)

CITY OF SAN RAMON COUNCIL MEMBERS AND DATES OF SERVICE

Name	**Dates of Service**
Jerry Aljouny	July 1983–April 1984
Richard Harmon	July 1983–November 1989
Diane Schinnerer	July 1983–November 1989
Wayne Bennett	July 1983–November 1991
Mary Lou Oliver	July 1983–November 1995
John Meakin	April 1984–November 1987
Fred Messreni	November 1987–November 1991
Barry Nudelman	November 1989–June 1991
Patricia Boom	November 1989–November 1997
Dennis Garrison	June 1991–November 1991
Jim Blickenstaff	November 1991–November 1993
Greg Carr	November 1991–November 1995
Hermann Welm	November 1991–November 1999
Curt Kinney	November 1993–November 2001

Name	Dates of Service
Ron Raab	November 1995–July 2001
David Hudson	November 1997–Present
Nancy Tatarka	November 1999–November 2003
H. Abram Wilson	November 1999–December 2011
Jim Livingstone	August 2001–November 2001
	January 2002–December 2013
Jerry Cambra	November 2001–December 2003
Donna Dickey	November 2001–November 2003
Scott Perkins	November 2003–Present
Carol Rowley	November 2003–December 2011
Bill Clarkson	December 2011–Present
Phil O'Loane	December 2011–Present
Harry Sachs	December 2013–Present

SAN RAMON MAYORS AND VICE MAYORS BY YEAR

In 2003, voters decided to elect mayors independently. The earlier mayors and vice mayors rotated into the positions.

Date	Mayor	Vice Mayor
7/1/83	Diane Schinnerer	Rick Harmon
4/17/84	Rick Harmon	Mary Lou Oliver
2/12/85	Mary Lou Oliver	Wayne Bennett
11/25/85	Wayne Bennett	John Meakin
11/19/86	John Meakin	Diane Schinnerer
11/10/87	Diane Schinnerer	Mary Lou Oliver
11/22/88	Wayne Bennett	Mary Lou Oliver
11/28/89	Mary Lou Oliver	Wayne Bennett

Date	Mayor	Vice Mayor
11/13/90	Wayne Bennett	Fred Messreni
11/26/91	Mary Lou Oliver	Patricia Boom
11/10/92	Patricia Boom	Hermann Welm
11/23/93	Hermann Welm	Greg Carr
11/22/94	Greg Carr	Curt Kinney
11/28/95	Curt Kinney	Patricia Boom
11/12/96	Patricia Boom	Hermann Welm
11/25/97	Hermann Welm	Byron Athan
11/24/98	Byron Athan	Curt Kinney
11/23/99	Curt Kinney	Ron Raab
11/28/00	Dave Hudson	Nancy Tatarka
11/27/01	Nancy Tatarka	H. Abram Wilson
11/26/02	H. Abram Wilson	Jerry Cambra
11/25/03	H. Abram Wilson	David Hudson
11/04/03	H. Abram Wilson	Jim Livingstone
11/29/05	H. Abram Wilson	Carol Rowley
11/06	H. Abram Wilson	Scott Perkins
11/07	H. Abram Wilson	Jim Livingstone
11/08	H. Abram Wilson	David Hudson
11/09	H. Abram Wilson	Carol Rowley
11/10	H. Abram Wilson	Scott Perkins
11/11	Bill Clarkson	Jim Livingstone
11/12	Bill Clarkson	Dave Hudson
11/13	Bill Clarkson	Phil O'Loane
11/14	Bill Clarkson	Harry Sachs
11/15	Bill Clarkson	Harry Sachs

SAN RAMON CITY MANAGERS

Name	Served From	Served To
George Gaekle	July 1983	September 1983
James Robinson	October 1983	December 1988
Byron Athan	December 1988	April 1989
Herb Moniz	May 1989	April 2002
Jim Randall	April 2002	December 2002
Gail Waiters	December 2002	May 2004
Byron Athan	May 2004	August 2004
Herb Moniz	August 2004	March 2011
Greg Rogers	April 2011	Present

SAN RAMON POST OFFICE AND POSTMASTERS

Name	Title	Date Appointed
Samuel Russell	Postmaster	11/20/1852
Discontinued on November 16, 1859		
Reestablished as SAN RAMOON on December 4, 1873		
Emery T. Mills	Postmaster	12/04/1873
Leo Lynch	Postmaster	07/10/1876
Changed to SAN RAMON on December 31, 1883		
Leo Lynch	Postmaster	12/31/1883
Henry C. Hurst	Postmaster	02/06/1884
Harry C. Hurst	Postmaster	08/18/1915
Mrs. Annie L. Fry	Postmaster	10/08/1924
Mrs. Percy R. DuBois	Acting Postmaster	10/08/1929
William C. Fereira	Acting Postmaster	01/27/1929
Byron J. Cochrane	Officer-In-Charge	06/20/1968
Crawford F. Smith	Postmaster	06/20/1977

Name	Title	Date Appointed
Claremont P. Allen	Officer-In-Charge	06/30/1977
Ronald C. Caggia	Officer-In-Charge	11/04/1977
Russell M. Teves	Postmaster	04/22/1978
Philip John Fraher	Officer-In-Charge	04/30/1982
James O. Evans	Postmaster	10/02/1982
Peter Chen	Postmaster	04/05/2003
Federick S. Crisostomo	Officer-In-Charge	06/03/2004
Guillermo L. Guzman	Officer-In-Charge	10/02/2004
Michael F. Benson	Postmaster	10/01/2005
Richard J. Martinez	Officer-In-Charge	04/21/2007
Richard J. Martinez	Postmaster	09/29/2007
Sonja Lewis	Officer-In-Charge	07/16/2008
Martin Nunez	Officer-In-Charge	10/01/2009
Martin Nunez	Postmaster	2/13/2010

Bibliography

A Look at San Ramon

Geldermann, Carmen. "The Story of San Ramon." *San Ramon Valley Old Timer*, May 1939.

Munro-Fraser, J.P. *History of Contra Costa County*. San Francisco, CA: W.A. Slocum, 1882, 429.

San Ramon General Plan, 1986.

Wiedemann, Henry. "San Ramon Memories." Unpublished manuscript, 1956. Museum of the San Ramon Valley.

First People: The Ohlone Indians

The Fages-Crespi Expedition of 1772. Pleasanton, CA: Amador-Livermore Historical Society, 1772. Translation of diaries written by Pedro Fages and Juan Crespi.

Milliken, Randall T. *A Time of Little Choice: The Disintegration of Tribal Culture in the San Francisco Bay Area, 1769–1810*. Menlo Park, CA: Ballena Press, 1995.

Ortiz, Bev. "Mount Diablo As Myth and Reality: An Indian History Convoluted," *American Indian Quarterly* (Fall 1989).

Powers, Stephen. *Tribes of California*. Berkeley: University of California Press, 1977, 109–10.

Jose Maria Amador's Rancho San Ramon

Alta California, September 22, 1860.
Amador, Jose Maria. *Recollections Concerning the History of California*. Written at the dictation of the author by Thomas Savage for the Bancroft Library, 1877, 78 and 95.
Oakland Daily Tribune. "A California Patriarch." Interviews with Jose Maria Amador by W.H. on May 22, 29 and June 3 and 10, 1875, available in the Oakland Public Library.

Early Pioneers Left Their Marks

Fereira, Chuck. Interview with the author, 2015, and Fereira genealogical information in Museum of the San Ramon Valley archives.
Gorthy, Richard. *The Christian Wiedemann Family History*. San Ramon, CA: Richard Gorthy, 2008.
Illustrations of Contra Costa Co., California, with Historical Sketch. Oakland, CA: Smith & Elliott, 1879. Reproduction by the Contra Costa County Historical Society. Sacramento, CA: Sacramento Lithograph Co., 1952.
Smith, James Dale. *Recollections, Early Life in the San Ramon Valley as Related by Prof. James Dale Smith Headmaster, Livermore College*. Oakland, CA: GRT Book Printing, 1995.
Munro-Fraser, J.P. *History of Contra Costa County*. San Francisco, CA: W.A. Slocum, 1882, 429.

San Ramon Could Have Been Limerick

Amador, Jose Maria. *Land Case 73, Northern District Court, 1955*. Bancroft Library, University of California–Berkeley.
Dotson, Irma. *San Ramon Branch Line of the Southern Pacific*. Danville, CA: Museum of the San Ramon Valley, 1991, 128–37.
Hoover, Mildred, Hero Eugene Rensch and Ethel Grace Rensch. *Historic Spots in California*. Stanford, CA: Stanford University Press, 1966, 57–58.
Munro-Fraser, J.P. *History of Contra Costa County*. San Francisco, CA: W.A. Slocum, 1882, 444.

Farmers and Ranchers of San Ramon

Banks, Peter M. and Joseph W. Morris. *Archaeological Investigation of the Cultural Resources within the Alamo Creek Planning Area, Contra Costa County, California*: Santina & Thompson, 1981, 14.

Boone, Ruth. Interview with the author, 1997.
Cozine, Ralph. *Agriculture: For a Century, the Business of the Valley*. Danville, CA: Museum of the San Ramon Valley, 2002.
Henry, Phil. Interview with the author, 2015.
Kaplan, Ann W. Interview. *San Ramon Valley Herald*, May 8, 1990.
Rasmussen, Gordon. Interview with the author, 2014.
Rutherford, Richard. "The $$$ Trend, Red and Black." *Valley Pioneer Centennial Edition*, September 4, 1958.
Wiedemann, Henry. "San Ramon Memories." Unpublished manuscript, 1956. Museum of the San Ramon Valley.
Wiedemann, Jeff. Interview. *San Ramon Valley Times*, June 16, 1975.
———. Interview with the author, 2015.
Wood, Don. "Random Recollections of Things I've Seen or Been Told." Unpublished manuscript, 2002. Museum of the San Ramon Valley.
———. Interview with the author, 2015.

San Ramon Scholars

Contra Costa Gazette, 1864, 1867 and April 11, 1874.
Fereira, Lee. "Fereira Played a Big Part in San Ramon." *Valley Pioneer*, June 26, 1968.
Museum of the San Ramon Valley archives.
Schulte, Irene. Letter, May 15, 1991. Museum of the San Ramon Valley archives.
Smith, James Dale. *Recollections, Early Life in the San Ramon Valley as Related by Prof. James Dale Smith Headmaster, Livermore College*. Oakland, CA: GRT Book Printing, 1995, 57.
Wiedemann, Sandee, ed. *Recollections of San Ramon, To Celebrate the 100th Birthday of the Permanent Naming of "San Ramon."* Unpublished compilation of historical materials, October 1991.

After the Civil War in San Ramon

Fereira, Bill. Interview. *Contra Costa Times*, July 1, 1998.
Munro-Fraser, J.P. *History of Contra Costa County*. San Francisco, CA: W.A. Slocum, 1882, 444.
Smith, James Dale. *Recollections, Early Life in the San Ramon Valley as Related by Prof. James Dale Smith Headmaster, Livermore College*. Oakland, CA: GRT Book Printing, 1995.
Wiedemann, Henry. "San Ramon Memories." Unpublished manuscript, 1956. Museum of the San Ramon Valley.

THE BOULEVARD'S GRANDE DAMES PLUS ONE

History of Contra Costa County, California with Biographical Sketches. Los Angeles: Historic Record Company, 1926, 175–76.

Hulaniski, F.J. *The History of Contra Costa County California*. Berkeley CA: Elms Publishing Co., 1917.

Illustrations of Contra Costa Co., California, with Historical Sketch. Oakland, CA: Smith & Elliott, 1879. Reproduction by the Contra Costa County Historical Society. Sacramento, CA: Sacramento Lithograph Co., 1952, 21 and 22.

Wiedemann, Henry. "San Ramon Memories." Unpublished manuscript, 1956. Museum of the San Ramon Valley.

AND HERE'S SAN RAMON—IN 1880

Contra Costa Gazette, March 9, 1880.

BISHOP RANCH IN THE HEART OF SAN RAMON

Boone, Ruth. Interview with author, 1997.

Contra Costa Gazette, Contra Costa Development Number. "Bishop Brothers—San Ramon Valley Ranch," 1916, 34.

"Frank Rutherford," 627–28. *History of Contra Costa County, California with Biographical Sketches.* Los Angeles: Historic Record Company, 1926.

San Ramon Valley Herald. "Last Ranch Manager Recalls Bishop Ranch," November 6, 1985.

San Ramon Valley Times, June 1, 1997; January 2, 2000.

Valley Pioneer, 1969–1970.

Valley Pioneer Centennial Edition. "Bishop Ranch, One of County's Finest," September 4, 1958.

Walnut Kernel. "San Ramon Rancho," August 1957, 31.

Wiedemann, Sandee, ed. *Recollections of San Ramon, To Celebrate the 100th Birthday of the Permanent Naming of "San Ramon."* October 1991, 11.

Wood, Don. "Random Recollections of Things I've Seen or Been Told." Unpublished manuscript, 2002. Museum of the San Ramon Valley.

HENRY WIEDEMANN'S SAN RAMON MEMORIES

Wiedemann, Henry. "San Ramon Memories." Unpublished manuscript, 1956. Museum of the San Ramon Valley.

The 1906 Earthquake and Fire Light Up the Western Sky

Daily Gazette-Martinez, 1906.

Davis, Bobbie. "The Quake in Contra Costa." In *A History of Contra Costa County*. Danville, CA: Tri-Valley, April–July 1976.

Lawson, Andrew C. *The California Earthquake of April 18, 1906. Report of the State Earthquake Investigation Commission*. Washington, D.C.: Carnegie Institution of Washington, 1908.

Ramona Park brochure, 1906.

The Twentieth Century Marches On

Boone, Ruth. Interview with author, July 29, 1997.

Buti, Bruno. *Jackass Brandy*. Cloverdale CA: Buti Publications, 1996.

Contra Costa County Dedication Day at the Pan-Pacific Exposition Program. April 3, 1915.

Davis, Bobbie. *A History of Contra Costa County*. Danville, CA: Tri-Valley News, April–July, 1976.

Fereira, Bill. Interview. *San Ramon Valley Times*, June 1, 1997; January 2, 2000.

Fereira, Viola. Interview. *San Ramon Valley Times*, January 2, 2000.

Henry, Jerry. Interview. *San Ramon Valley Times*, June 1, 1997.

Kaplan, Ann. Interview with the author, September 25, 1996.

Oliver, Mary Lou. Interview with the author, 2015.

San Ramon Valley Chamber brochure, 1965.

Schinnerer, Diane. *Oakland Tribune*, 1983.

The Party Place: San Ramon Hall

Contra Costa Gazette, January 11, 1896, 1911.

Fereira, Bill. Interview. *Herald/News*, August 18, 1974

Geldermann, Carmen. "The Story of San Ramon." *San Ramon Valley Old Timer*, May 1, 1939.

Herald/News, August 18, 1974.

Museum of the San Ramon Valley archives.

Walnut Kernel, 1941.

Rose Peters Emery's Recollections

Emery, Rose Peters. *Footprints in the Soil, A Portuguese-Californian Remembers*. San Jose, CA: Portuguese Heritage Publications, 2003.

LIBRARIES, PAST AND PRESENT

Camacho, Winky. Interview with the author, 2013.
Contra Costa County Library Long Range Plan, 1988–1991, 1–2, 11–20.
Danville Grange # 85. Minute Books. January 2, 1909, November 20, 1909 and March 5, 1910.
Emery, Rose Peters. *Footprints in the Soil, A Portuguese-Californian Remembers*. San Jose, CA: Portuguese Heritage Publications, 2003, 108, 118.
Jones, Virgie V. *Historical Persons and Places…in San Ramon Valley*. Alamo, CA: Morris-Burt Press, 1977.
Kaplan, Ann Wiedemann. Interview with the author. 1996.
Kreiser, Nancy. Interview with the author. 2015.
News Notes of California Libraries, April 1926, 137. Museum of the San Ramon Valley archives.
Parks, Barbara. Interview with the author. 2007.
Schinnerer, Diane. Interview with the author. 2015
Soto, Bill. Interview with the author. 2007.
Soto, Gary. Interview with the author. 2011.
Tri-Valley News. "Lack of Interest Stymies San Ramon Library," August 2, 1974.
Valley Pioneer. "Library 'Seed' Planted," March 27, 1985.

SAN RAMON WELCOMES THE FREEWAY IN 1966

DD brochure. Museum of the San Ramon Valley archives.
Dehaesus, Tony. Interview with the author. 1997.
Kaplan, Al. Interview with the author, August 30, 1997.
May, Margaret. Interview with the author. 1991.
Valley Pioneers, 1962–1966.

SAN RAMON'S FIRE PROTECTION DISTRICT, 1963–80

Contra Costa Times, December 13, 1979.
Deardorff, Mel. Interview with the author. August 22, 2008.
Fereira, Bill. Interview with the author. March 21, 1997, 2008.
Museum of the San Ramon Valley archives.
Probert, Rick. Interview with the author. 2008.
San Ramon Valley Fire Protection District. *Fire Line*. Booklet published by SRVFPD, 1987.
Tri-Valley News, December 19, 1979.
Valley Pioneers, 1963–80. Weekly newspapers.

SUBURBAN SAN RAMON—SOUTH

Athan, Byron. Interview with the author. 1997.

———. *San Ramon Valley Times*, September 17, 1988.

Fahey, Dick. Interview with the author. 1997.

Fereira, Chuck. Interview with the author. 2015.

Henry, Chuck. Interview with the author. 2015

Independent, June 11, 1975.

Lee, Ed, and Carol Lee. Interview with the author. 2015.

Schinnerer, Diane, and Don Schinnerer. Interview with the author. 2015.

Sprouse, Dale and Sue Stephenson. *Dublin San Ramon Services District: The First 50 Years 1953–2003*. San Ramon, CA: San Ramon Services District, Human Resources Department, 2003.

Valley Pioneer, 1960–88. Weekly newspapers.

Vonheeder-Leopold, Georgene. Interview with the author. 2015.

Wahlig, Mike, and Joyce Wahlig. Interview with the author. 2015.

SUBURBAN SAN RAMON—NORTH

Coleman, Dan, Jr. Interview with the author. 2015.

Covello, Joe. Interview with the author. 2015.

Fereira, Bill. Interview with the author. June 22, 2007.

Mehran, Alex. Interview with the author. 2015.

Schinnerer, Diane, and Don Schinnerer. Interview with the author. 2015.

Valley Pioneer. "San Ramon…A Decade of Progress." Supplement, Spring 1967; 1965–81.

Western Electric Master Plan report and map, 1971.

BISHOP RANCH BUSINESS PARK

Bishop Ranch Business Park brochures and magazines, including the *Special 50th Anniversary Edition, Bishop Ranch City Center*, 2014.

Boone, Ruth. Interview with the author. 1997.

Coleman, Dan, Jr. Interview with the author. 2015.

Gonzales, Neil. "Bishop Ranch's City Center Project to Bring Newfound Downtown in San Ramon." *The Registry for Bay Area Real Estate*. February 27, 2015. http://news.theregistrysf.com/.

Kallam, Clay. "The Birth of the Cool." *Diablo Magazine*, May 2015.

Mehran, Alex. Interview with the author. 2015.

———. "Bishop Ranch—A Twenty Year Perspective." Lecture, October 22, 1997.

Mehran, Alexander, Jr. "Renzo Piano to Design San Ramon's City Center at Bishop Ranch." *The Registry for Bay Area Real Estate*, June 3, 2014. http://news.theregistrysf.com/.

Oliver, Mary Lou. Interview with the author. 2015.

San Francisco Business Times. "The Future of Bishop Ranch," June 21, 2013.

San Ramon Valley Times. "Orchard Became Fertile Ground for Business," April 28, 1991.

Schinnerer, Diane. Interview with the author, 2015.

Sunset Development Company. *Bishop Ranch: The Best Place to Build a Business*. N.p., 2002.

———. *Bishop Ranch*, N.p., 2011.

Truebridge, Chris. Interview with the author. 2015.

Valley Pioneer, 1978–88. Weekly newspaper.

Wahlig, Mike, and Joyce Wahlig. Interview with the author. 2015.

Wiedemann, Jeff. Interview with the author. 2015.

The Dougherty Valley

Ambruster, Ariel. "Battle of Dougherty Valley Approaches Landmark Truce." *San Ramon Valley Times*, May 14, 1995.

———. "Dougherty Valley Developer Settles for Delta Water." *San Ramon Valley Times*, June 23, 1995.

Bennett, Virginia. *Dublin Reflections*. Dublin, CA: Friends of the Dublin Library, 1978.

Eorio, Jeff. Interview with the author. 2015.

Greiger, Tom. "Dougherty Plan Splits San Ramon." *San Ramon Valley Times*, September 6, 1992.

Museum of the San Ramon Valley archives.

Oliver, Mary Lou. Interview with the author. 2015.

Truebridge, Chris. Interview with the author. 2015.

Wong, Phil. Interview with the author. 2015.

San Ramon Embraces Cityhood

Athan, Byron. Interview with the author. 1997.

Covello, Joe. Interview with the author. 2015.

Horvath, Alex. "The Past: Where It All Began." *San Ramon Valley Herald*. San Ramon 20th Anniversary Celebration, July 2003, 5.

Oliver, Mary Lou. Interview with the author. 2015.

Schinnerer, Diane, and Don Schinnerer. Interview with the author. 2015.

Valley Pioneers, 1979–85.

Wahlig, Mike, and Joyce Wahlig. Interview with the author. 2015.
Zion, William R. "The San Ramon Incorporation Feasibility Study." Unpublished report, Museum of the San Ramon Valley November 1981.

THE CITY'S FIRST DECADES

Athan, Byron. Interview with the author. 1997
Clarkson, Bill. Interview with the author. 2015.
Covello, Joe. Interview with the author. 2015.
Hershenson, Karen, and Al Goodman. "San Ramon a City; New Council Elected." *Contra Costa Times*, March 9, 1983.
Horvath, Alex. "Community, Schools Work Hand in Hand." *San Ramon Valley Herald*, San Ramon 20th Anniversary Celebration, Special edition, July 2003, 18.
———. "Sacrifices Key to Incorporation." *San Ramon Valley Herald*, San Ramon 20th Anniversary Celebration, Special edition, July 2003, 11.
———. "San Ramon Facing a Variety of Issues." *San Ramon Valley Herald*. San Ramon 20th Anniversary Celebration, July 2003, 20.
San Ramon Valley Times. 1982.
Schinnerer, Diane. Interview with the author, 2015.
Schinnerer, Don. Interview with the author, 2015.
Valley Pioneer, 1982–83.
Wahlig, Mike. Interview with the author, 2015.
Wong, Phil. Interview with the author, 2015.

WHERE *IS* SAN RAMON?

Clarkson, Bill. Interview with the author. 2015.
Covello, Joe. "The Past: Where It All Began," *San Ramon Valley Herald*. San Ramon 20th Anniversary Celebration, July 2003, 5.
Horvath, Alex. "San Ramon Facing a Variety of Issues." *San Ramon Valley Herald*. San Ramon 20th Anniversary Celebration, July 2003, 20.
Kallam, Clay. "Birth of the Cool." *Diablo Magazine*, May 2015.
Mehran, Alex. Interview with the author. 2015.
Mehran, Alexander, Jr. "Renzo Piano to Design San Ramon's City Center at Bishop Ranch." *The Registry for Bay Area Real Estate*, June 3, 2014. http://news.theregistrysf.com/.
O'Loane, Phil. Interview with the author. 2015.
Schinnerer, Diane, and Don Schinnerer. Interview with the author. 2015.
Valley Pioneer, January 5 and 26, 1983.
Wong, Phil. Interview with the author. 2015.

ADDITIONAL SOURCES

Beck, Warren, and Ynez Haase. *Historical Atlas of California*. Norman: University of Oklahoma Press, 1975.

Contra Costa County Historical Society, History Center archives.

Crane, Ron, and Kevin Crane. *Geology of the San Ramon Valley: A Personal Account of the Present Geologic Knowledge of the Area*. Computer-produced and illustrated, 2002. 65 pp. Museum of San Ramon Valley archives.

Emanuels, George. *California's Contra Costa County, An Illustrated History*. Fresno, CA: Panorama West Books, 1986.

Harlan, Jake. *California '46–'88*. San Francisco: Bancroft Co., 1888.

Jones, Virgie V. *Be It Ever So Humble*. Alamo, CA: Morris-Burt Press, 1983.

———. *Historical Persons & Places…In San Ramon Valley*. Alamo, CA: Morris-Burt Press, 1977.

Laffey, Glory Anne. *Historic Architectural Survey Report for Fostoria Way Overpass Project*. Public Affairs Management, 1990.

Leykam, John. *Contra Costa County: A Chronicle of Progress*. Northridge, CA: Windsor Publications, 1989.

Lindsay, Roxanne Wiedemann. "San Ramon—A Brief History." *San Ramon Chamber of Commerce Directory*, 1986.

Museum of the San Ramon Valley archives.

Purcell, Mae Fisher. *History of Contra Costa County*. Berkeley, CA: Gillick Press, 1946.

Scott, Edna Lynch. *A San Ramon Rancher's Wife, Minnie Gray Coxhead Lynch*. Unpublished booklet at the Museum of the San Ramon Valley 2004.

Wells, A.J. *Contra Costa County California*. San Francisco, CA: Sunset Homeseekers' Bureau, 1912.

Wollenberg, Charles. *Golden Gate Metropolis: Perspectives on Bay Area History*. University of California–Berkeley Institute of Government Studies, 1985.

Index

D

E

F

About the Author

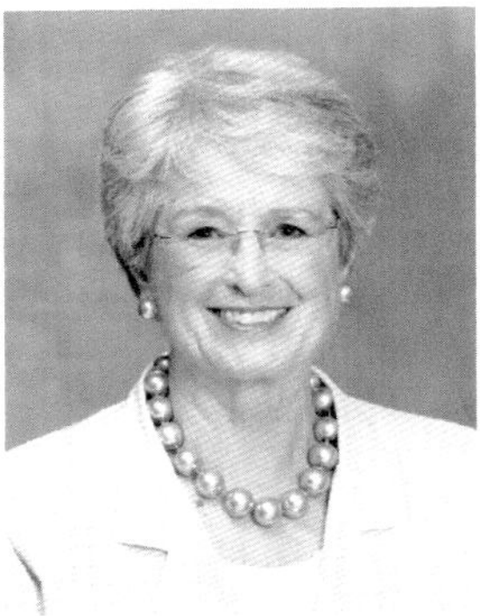

Beverly Lane was raised, schooled, married and lived in California. She has witnessed communities change from pastoral orchards to suburbs both in Orange County and in the San Ramon Valley. Beverly attended Occidental College in Los Angeles, which produced many California historians, from Robert G. Cleland, Andrew F. Rolle and (her classmate) Richard Orsi. While they wrote about a larger stage, her focus has been local California history—in particular, the San Ramon Valley, where she and her family have lived for over forty years.

A teacher and an Oakland Museum docent, Beverly is a former mayor of Danville. She is currently an elected director on the East Bay Regional Park District board and curator of the Museum of the San Ramon Valley.

She has written numerous newspaper columns and three books: *San Ramon Valley—Alamo, Danville, San Ramon* (an Arcadia Publishing book with Ralph Cozine); *Vintage Danville* (a sesquicentennial history with Laura Grinstead); and *Before BART: Electric Railroads Link Contra Costa County*. *San Ramon Chronicles* will provide an opportunity for readers to learn about this vibrant, twenty-first-century city.